Light
on
Great Bible Themes

Light
on
Great Bible Themes

by

HUGH R. HORNE

WILLIAM B. EERDMANS PUBLISHING COMPANY
GRAND RAPIDS, MICHIGAN

Dedication

to

DR. PAUL EDWARD ROBERTS

who was the officiant at my baptism, my ordination to the gospel ministry, and our wedding. He has always exemplified the spirit of Christ in his daily walk, and his life has been a constant source of inspiration and blessing to me.

and to

ELLIS G. YOES

faithful deacon and pastor's friend.

Introduction

The sermonic menu of the twentieth century has specialized in dietary delicacies. It is thus gratifying to see a volume dedicated to more meaty theology. The growing Christian needs doctrine like the body needs protein, and this group of sermons is aimed at the task of raising Christians from an adolescence into a maturity that is so desperately needed in our churches today. For this is a day when the pulpit is answering questions no one is asking. The trumpet too often gives an uncertain sound, but Pastor Horne has raised the gospel trumpet to his lips and sounded a call for clear thinking and dynamic beliefs.

The subjects that he deals with are vital to the foundations of the Christian faith. The reasoning is clear, the substance is Biblical, and the application is practical. He has laid the axe at the roots of the tree; he is dealing with basic cures, not simply treating the symptoms. I have perused these pages with delightful admiration, and I know that they will bless and strengthen the minds and hearts that they will touch. There is no substitute for truth dressed in the garments of humble talent.

The word of God is the common denominator of all knowledge. I recommend these sermons because they adhere to the teachings of the Book. These are not vain babblings that sound like noisy brass or a tinkling cymbal. They are anchored to Christ and yet geared to the times. I pray that God will anoint them with oil of the Holy Spirit so that they will return not void but filled, accomplishing the purpose for which they were sent.

—ANGEL MARTINEZ, *Evangelist*

Preface

A well-known editor recently wrote an article in which he decried the dearth of doctrinal preaching in our churches today. With this in mind, I prepared and preached these sermons in the church I serve as pastor. The results testified to the fact that people need and desire such teaching.

I am grateful to many sources for help in preparing these sermons. Acknowledgements of authors and publishers are listed elsewhere in this book.

I am deeply indebted to my beloved wife, Faye, who has always been a real inspiration to me in my work; to Mrs. Ralph Pearman, my sister, who typed the final draft of the manuscript as a labor of love; and to Angel Martinez, evangelist and writer, who wrote the Introduction. I have the privilege of serving as his pastor.

This book is sent forth with the sincere desire and fervent prayer that it may help many to know Christ and to love his precious word. — HUGH ROBERT HORNE

Contents

CHAPTER ONE

Incarnation: "Joy to the World"

> "But made himself of no reputation, and took upon
> himself the form of a servant, and was made in
> the likeness of men" (Philippians 2:7).
> "And the Word was made flesh, and dwelt among
> us" (John 1:14).

A LITTLE CHILD was left in the darkness after his mother had
put him to bed and turned out the light. "Am I going to be left
alone in the dark?" he anxiously cried. "Yes, my dear," his
mother replied, "but you have God with you all the time."
Quickly the child answered, "Yes, I know God is here, but I
want someone who has a face."

God has given us Christ to reveal his face to us!

Lewis Sperry Chafer has said:

> The Bible presents many contrasts, but none more striking than
> that one person should be at the same time very God and very
> man. Illustrations . . . of these contrasts are many: he was
> weary, yet he called the weary to himself for rest. He was hungry,
> yet he was "the bread of life." He was thirsty, yet he was "the
> water of life." He was in agony, yet he healed all manner of
> disease and soothed every pain. He "grew, and waxed strong in
> spirit," yet he was from all eternity. He was tempted, yet he,
> as God, could not be tempted. He became self-limited in knowl-
> edge, yet he was the wisdom of God. . . .He prayed, yet he an-
> swered prayer. He wept at the tomb, yet he called the dead to
> arise. . . .He died, yet he is eternal life. He was God's ideal
> man, and man's ideal God.[1]

1 Lewis Sperry Chafer, *Major Bible Themes*, pp. 34-35.

There are four facts relative to this doctrine which we shall notice here: the *pledge*, the *proof*, the *perpetuity*, and the *purposes* of the incarnation. Before we develop these thoughts in detail, however, we offer Dr. P. B. Fitzwater's concise definition of the incarnation:

> By the incarnation is meant that in the person of Jesus Christ the eternal God embodied himself and tabernacled among men; the divine and human natures interpenetrating, thereby becoming one. It was not the divine nature filling the human, as an empty vessel is filled, but the divine Person taking up within himself the human nature, thus becoming the God-man.[2]

I. THE PLEDGE OF THE INCARNATION

1. *The Old Testament recounts the pledge.* Isaiah predicted, "Therefore, the Lord himself shall give you a sign; behold, a virgin shall conceive, and bear a son, and shall call his name Immanuel" (Isaiah 7:14). Again he gives us that immortal prophecy in the ninth chapter: "For unto us a child is born, unto us a son is given; and the government shall be upon his shoulder; and his name shall be called Wonderful, Counsellor, The mighty God, The everlasting Father, The Prince of Peace" (Isaiah 9:6). Micah also prophesies concerning Christ's coming: "But thou, Bethlehem Ephratah, though thou be little among the thousands of Judah, yet out of thee shall he come forth unto me that is to be ruler in Israel; whose goings forth have been from of old, from everlasting" (Micah 5:2).

These men, inspired by God, here foretell the coming of Christ in the flesh some eight hundred years before he appeared.

Old Testament characters, in many instances, typify the coming and ministry of the God-man:

Moses, as a prophet, is a type of Christ. Both were sent by God; both spoke God's word; both wrought miracles in evidence; and both were rejected by Israel.

Jonah is a type of Christ in his resurrection.

Adam is a "figure of him which was to come" (Romans 5:14). Samson, Joshua and David, in their victories, typify Christ as the great Victor.

2 P. B. Fitzwater, *When God Became Man*, p. 3.

Joseph is the great character type of the Lord Jesus. Each was beloved by his father (Genesis 37:3; Matthew 3:17); each was sent to his brethren (Genesis 37:12-13; John 1:11); each was hated by his brethren (Genesis 37:4, 8, 18; John 7:7; Matthew 12:14); each was rejected by his brethren (Genesis 37:8; John 19:15); each was delivered to death (Genesis 37:18, 23-24; Acts 2:22-23); each was raised from the grave (Genesis 37:28; Acts 2:23-24, 27); each took a Gentle bride (Genesis 41:45; Acts 15:14; Ephesians 5:25); each delivered Israel (Genesis 45:3, 7; Romans 11:25-26).

Abel and his sacrifice is another Old Testament picture of Jesus. Abel offered a divinely appointed sacrifice; Christ was a divinely appointed sacrifice. Abel offered a flawless sacrifice; Christ was a perfect sacrifice. Abel offered a sacrifice of blood; Christ gave his own blood in sacrifice. Abel offered an acceptable sacrifice; Christ was an acceptable sacrifice. Abel offered a temporarily effective sacrifice; Christ was an eternally sufficient sacrifice.

The Old Testament tabernacle and Noah's ark are further types of Christ. These and others illustrate God's pledge that Christ would tabernacle among men.

2. *The New Testament records his incarnation.* "God was manifest in the flesh . . ." (I Timothy 3:16). ". . . Christ Jesus: who, being in the form of God, thought it not robbery to be equal with God; but made himself of no reputation, and took upon him the form of a servant, and was made in the likeness of men" (Philippians 2:5-7).

A group of missionaries, whose compound was near the royal palace, heard a loud noise over the wall in the palace grounds. Investigating, they found that the young prince, to whom they had earlier given a song book after singing him Christmas hymns, had his fat gentlemen-in-waiting lined up in a pavilion demanding that they sing. "The joyful noise is in that book, and you've got to get it out!" he commanded.

The joyful news is that God in Christ came into the world and identified himself with man — miraculously, conceived by the Holy Ghost and born of a virgin!

The New Testament declares that angels *announced* his birth.

"And she shall bring forth a Son, and thou shalt call his name Jesus; for he shall save his people from their sins" (Matthew 1: 21). ". . . Thou shalt . . . bring forth a Son, and shalt call his name Jesus" (Luke 1:31). "And the angel of the Lord . . . said unto them, Fear not, for, behold, I bring you good tidings of great joy. . . . For unto you is born . . . a Saviour, which is Christ the Lord" (Luke 2:9-11).

The New Testament discloses that shepherds *acknowledged* him at his birth. "And they came with haste and found . . . the babe lying in a manger. And when they had seen it, they made known abroad . . . concerning this child. And the shepherds returned, glorifying and praising God" (Luke 2:16-17, 20).

The New Testament describes how the wise men *adored* him at his birth. ". . . there came wise men . . . saying, Where is he that is born King of the Jews? for we have seen his star in the east and have come to worship him" (Matthew 2:1-2).

The New Testament divulges that Herod was *annoyed* because of his birth. "When Herod the king had heard these things, he was troubled" (Matthew 2:3).

The New Testament discusses how wise men today may *accept* him. "That if thou shalt confess with thy mouth the Lord Jesus, and shalt believe in thine heart that God hath raised him from the dead, thou shalt be saved" (Romans 10:9).

While walking in his garden one day with a friend, Alfred Lord Tennyson was asked, "What do you think of Jesus Christ?" Tennyson pointed to a beautiful flower and said, "As the sun is to that flower, so Jesus Christ is to me."

God kept his pledge: Christ came in the fullness of time; and because of his supernatural birth, his sinless life, his sacrificial death on the cross, and his significant resurrection from the dead, his salvation is offered to every man.

II. *THE PROOFS OF THE INCARNATION*

1. *The works of Christ prove that he is God incarnate.* ". . . for the works which the Father hath given me to finish, the same works that I do, bear witness of me, that the Father hath sent me" (John 5:36). "And many other signs truly did Jesus . . . which are not written in this book; but these are written,

that ye might believe that Jesus is the Son of God" (John 20:30-31).

Great works have been performed by great men, but none can compare with the miraculous works of Jesus Christ! His mighty works include his miraculous birth, his sinless life, and his willing death, as well as the miracles which he performed during his public ministry. He healed the sick; he raised the dead; he changed the very laws of nature.

This miracle of Christ has been related in many ways. One has said of him:

> More than nineteen hundred years ago there was a Man born contrary to the laws of life. This Man lived in poverty and was reared in obscurity. He did not travel extensively. Only once did he cross the boundary of the country in which he lived; that was during his exile in childhood.
>
> He possessed neither wealth nor influence. His relatives were inconspicuous, and had neither training nor formal education.
>
> In infancy he startled a king; in childhood he puzzled doctors; in manhood he ruled the course of nature, walked upon the billows as if pavements, and hushed the sea to sleep.
>
> He healed the multitudes without medicine and made no charge for his service.
>
> He never wrote a book, and yet all the libraries of the country could not hold the books that have been written about him.
>
> He never wrote a song, and yet he has furnished the theme for more songs than all the songwriters combined.
>
> He never founded a college, but all the schools put together cannot boast of having as many students.
>
> He never marshaled an army, nor drafted a soldier, nor fired a gun; and yet no leader ever had more volunteers who have, under his orders, made more rebels stack arms and surrender without a shot fired.
>
> He never practiced medicine, and yet he has healed more broken hearts than all the doctors far and near.
>
> Every seventh day the wheels of commerce cease their turning and multitudes wend their way to worshiping assemblies to pay homage and respect to him.
>
> The names of the past proud statesmen of Greece and Rome have come and gone. The names of the past scientists, philosophers, and theologians have come and gone; but the name of this Man abounds more and more. Though time has spread nineteen hundred years between the people of this generation and the scene of his crucifixion, yet he still lives. Herod could not destroy him, and the grave could not hold him.

He stands forth upon the highest pinnacle of heavenly glory, proclaimed of God, acknowledged by angels, adored by saints, and feared by devils, as the living, personal Christ, our Lord and Saviour.[3]

Several years ago the king of England visited America, and while returning to Britain his ship encountered one of the worst storms ever recorded on the Atlantic Ocean. It is told that the king walked the decks of the British man-of-war during that storm, for he had been trained in the ways of seamanship. But even though he was considered the greatest king on earth, he could not still the raging waves of the tempest. Only Jesus could do that! (Luke 8:22-24). Such are the mighty works of Jesus!

2. *The words of Christ prove that he is God incarnate.* "Never man spake like this man" (John 7:46). ". . . The words that I speak unto you I speak not of myself; but the Father that dwelleth in me" (John 14:10). His pertinent illustrations, his unusual metaphors, and the deep meaning of such discourses as the Sermon on the Mount are unexcelled by the combined writings of all great literary men. He himself never wrote a book, yet his teachings have endured for almost 2,000 years.

William Edward Biederwolf has said of Christ's preaching:

Take the teachings of Jesus Christ about the great fundamental ethical conceptions, such as love and truth and purity and duty, and where in any non-Christian religion or when on the lips of any non-Christian teacher did the world ever see or hear moral philosophy so profound, so radiant with divine glory and so God-like as that which came from the heart and mind of this marvelous Man of Galilee.[4]

3. *The resurrection of Christ proves that he is God incarnate.* Jesus Christ is "declared to be the Son of God with power, according to the spirit of holiness, by the resurrection from the dead" (Romans 1:3-4). He laid down his life knowing that "I have power to lay it down, and I have power to take it again" (John 10:17-18).

Most of the religions of the world claim special virtues for their leaders or their gods; but only Christianity can ever lay

---

3 *The Incomparable Christ* (Author unknown).
4 William Edward Biederwolf, *Evangelistic Sermons,* p. 20.

claim to resurrection. It is said that a young man once decided to found a new religion and went to a philosopher for advice. "What claims do you have as a great religious leader?" the wise man inquired. When the young man declared that he had none, the older man said: "If you will die, and after several days arise from the dead, you will be able to claim many followers; for this is what Jesus Christ did and he has millions who follow him."

III. *THE PERPETUITY OF THE INCARNATION*

The incarnation is not a single event; it is a continuing testimony of God's power and grace:

Romans 6:9 indicates that Christ will retain his human body forever.

1 Timothy 2:5, referring to the mediatorship of Jesus Christ in heaven at present, declares that he is "the man Christ Jesus."

Hebrews 13:8 reveals "Jesus Christ the same yesterday, and today, and forever."

During his time on earth until his death on the cross, he permitted certain human limitations in his body; for he was hungry (Matthew 4:2; 21:18), and he was thirsty (John 19:28); he was weary (John 4:6), and he slept (Matthew 8:24); he was subject to his parents (Luke 2:51), and he was subject to men's laws (Matthew 17:24-27); and he suffered.

After his resurrection, however, he possessed a glorified body, and it is in this body that he is now present in heaven (Acts 1:9; Ephesians 4:9-10).

IV. *THE PURPOSES OF THE INCARNATION*

1. *The purpose of his incarnation is to reveal the essence of God.* Jesus declared that "he that hath seen me hath seen the Father" (John 14:9). Hebrews 1:3 tells us that Christ is the express image of the person of God.

If we would learn of the *holiness* of God, we look to Jesus, of whom it was said that there was no sin in him.

If we would learn of the *love* of God, we look to Jesus, of whom it was said that he died for us while we were his enemies (Romans 5:10).

If we would learn of the *compassion* of God, we look to Jesus, who wept over an indifferent city filled with sinners; and who was moved with compassion as he looked upon the multitude as sheep without a shepherd.

If we would know the *forgiving spirit* of God, we look to Jesus who cried, "Father, forgive them" (Luke 23:34).

If we would know something of the *judgment* of God which must eventually come upon all sin and every form of wickedness, we look to Jesus, into whose hands will be entrusted this judgment (Psalm 2:6-9).

2. *The purpose of his incarnation is to reckon what man should be.* His life was an example of perfect manhood, and we are told to walk as he walked. "For even hereunto were ye called; because Christ also suffered for us, leaving us an example, that ye should follow his steps" (1 Peter 2:21). "He that saith he abideth in him ought himself also so to walk, even as he walked" (I John 2:6). Jesus says in John 13:15, "For I have given you an example, that ye should do as I have done to you."

Since Christ is all things to the believer, it is not only possible for the believer to walk in Christ, but God expects him to do so.

Christ is the *source* of our life (Ephesians 2:1; Galatians 2:20).

Christ is the *sustenance* of our life (John 6:51).

He is the *solace* of our life (Hebrews 13:5).

He is the *sphere* of our life (Philippians 1:21).

Hs is the *standard* of our life (Philippians 2:5).

He is the *satisfaction* of our life (I John 3:2).

3. *The purpose of his incarnation is to redeem us by his death.* ". . . we are sanctified by the offering of the body of Jesus Christ once for all" (Hebrews 10:10). "He that committeth sin is of the devil; for the devil sinneth from the beginning. For this purpose the Son of God was manifested, that he might destroy the works of the devil" (I John 3:8). "Forasmuch then as the children are partakers of flesh and blood, he also himself likewise took part of the same; that through death he might destroy him that had the power of death, that is, the devil; and deliver them who through fear of death were all their lifetime subject to bondage" (Hebrews 2:14-15).

"The *fear* of death was ours; the *power* of death was Satan's; the *taste* and *suffering* of death were Christ's. Through the *medium* of death Christ destroyed not only death itself, but also him that had the power of death."

Through the redeeming power of Christ J. W. Jowett's words bear real significance: "Death is not the end; it is only the beginning. Death is not the master of the house; he is only the porter at the King's lodge, appointed to open the gate and let the King's guests into the realm of eternal day. And so shall we ever be with the Lord."

When Christ redeems us he makes an eternal claim upon us. In a small village a cottage caught on fire, and since there was no fire engine, the house was soon enveloped in flames. Realizing that the occupants of the house were still inside a young man rushed into the flames and soon returned with two small children. But before he could re-enter the cottage to rescue the parents, the roof caved in and they were trapped in the flames. The young man was severely burned in the rescue, and it was some time before he was able to be about again. Soon the town council met in order to decide what was to be done with the children. There were two who claimed them and offered them a home. One was the squire of the village, a man of wealth and position. The other was the young man who had saved them. When asked what right he had to the little ones, he held up his hands which had been burned and scarred for them. Christ suffered in the flesh to redeem and claim us.

4. *The purpose of his incarnation is to represent us as our High Priest.* ". . . it behooved him to be made like unto his brethren, that he might be a merciful and faithful high priest in things pertaining to God, to make reconciliation for the sins of the people" (Hebrews 2:17). "For we have not an high priest which cannot be touched with the feeling of our infirmities; but was in all points tempted like as we are, yet without sin" (Hebrews 4:15).

Christ becomes our mediator, our go-between, before God. Mr. Moody asked a lad to bring his umbrella to him, and in doing so the boy fell and broke the umbrella. He was afraid, and he prevailed upon his parents to break the news to Mr.

Moody, which they did. The preacher then said to the boy: "When you broke my umbrella, you became frightened and ashamed, didn't you? Then you thought, if I tell mother or father, they can go between me and Mr. Moody and straighten things up. Now that your father has straightened things up, you can come to me. Now, my lad, that is the way it is with all of us; we are sinners — afraid of God. But God has provided a Mediator — someone to go between us and him — Jesus."

CHAPTER TWO

Deity: "Great God Our King"

"In the beginning was the Word, and the Word was with God, and the Word was God. The same was in the beginning with God" (John 1:1-2).

WHILE DINING WITH a group of literary men in Boston, Daniel Webster turned the conversation to the subject of Christianity. He frankly stated his belief in the divinity of Christ and his dependence upon the atonement of the Saviour. When he had paused, one of the men present said, "Mr. Webster, can you comprehend how Christ could be both God and man?" Webster promptly replied, "No, sir, I cannot comprehend it. If I could comprehend him, he would be no greater than myself. I feel that I need a superhuman Saviour."

The Old Testament *affirms* Christ to be God; angels *announce* him to be God; demons *acknowledge* him to be God; the Father *addresses* him as God; the Holy Spirit *assures* us he is God; he himself *avers* he is God; the New Testament *asserts* that he is God; myriad multitudes *avow* him to be God; and the whole universe shall *acclaim* him as God.

1. *The Old Testament Affirms Him To Be God.* Isaiah prophesies in 7:14: "Therefore the Lord himself shall give you a sign; behold, a virgin shall conceive, and bear a son, and shall call his name Immanuel."

Isaiah then prophesies concerning John the Baptist and his coming mission: "The voice of him that crieth in the wilderness, Prepare ye the way of the Lord, make straight in the desert a highway for our God" (40:3). This is fulfilled, according to

23

the record in Matthew: "In those days came John the Baptist. . . . For this is he that was spoken of by the prophet Esaias, saying, The voice of one crying in the wilderness, Prepare ye the way of the Lord, make his paths straight" (3:1, 3). Malachi foretells John's preparing of the way for the Christ (3:1).

Again, the prophet Isaiah tells of the coming of Christ, and speaks of him as God: "For unto us a child is born, unto us a son is given; and the government shall be upon his shoulder; and his name shall be called Wonderful, Counsellor, The mighty God, The everlasting Father, The Prince of Peace" (9:6).

Zechariah speaks concerning Christ (13:7), and Jesus himself refers to this prophecy in Matthew 26:31.

A Jewish girl, reading the Old Testament scriptures, inquired of her father concerning these prophecies. "Do you not recognize in Jesus the Promised One?" she said to him.

"Ah, no!" her father cried. "To be sure, the prophet speaks of the Messiah, but he has not yet appeared."

The young lady however, continued to study the verses, and ultimately the Holy Spirit opened her eyes, and she gave her heart and life to Jesus the Messiah. "There is no doubt about it," she now testifies. "Jesus is truly God's holy Son."

2. *Angels Announce Him To Be God.* The wonderful story in Luke is familiar to almost everyone. The shepherds stood in awe as the glory of the Lord shone around them. Then they saw the angel, who said: "Fear not; for, behold, I bring you good tidings of great joy, which shall be to all people. For unto you is born this day in the city of David a Saviour, which is Christ the Lord" (Luke 2:10-11).

Matthew records the angel's words to Mary after the resurrection, announcing him as God: ". . . Fear not ye: for I know that ye seek Jesus . . . He is not here; for he is risen, as he said. Come see the place where the Lord lay" (Matthew 28:5-6). The title "*the* Lord" belongs only to God. Acts 4:26 verifies this: "The kings of the earth stood up, and the rulers were gathered together against the Lord, and against his Christ."

The writer of Hebrews tells us that the angels were to worship him as God. ". . . When he bringeth in the firstbegotten into the world, he saith, And let all the angels of God worship him" (1:6).

Thus the angels can do nothing else but announce to the whole world that Jesus Christ is God!

3. *Demons Acknowledge Him To Be God.* Mark records the account of a man possessed with an unclean spirit. The demons cried out and said, "Let us alone; what have we to do with thee, thou Jesus of Nazareth? Art thou come to destroy us? I know thee who thou art, the Holy One of God" (1:24).

In Matthew we have recorded the story of two who were possessed with devils. The demons cried out when Jesus came near, "What have we to do with thee, Jesus, thou Son of God? Art thou come hither to torment us before the time?" (8:29). The term "Son of God" as applied to Christ indicates his full deity. As Son of God the Father, he is equal with God (John 5:18).

The Father Addresses Him As God. God is speaking of Jesus as God in Hebrews 1:8: "But unto the Son he saith, Thy throne, O God, is forever and ever; a sceptre of righteousness is the sceptre of thy kingdom."

He continues to speak of Jesus in Hebrews 1:10, showing that he was in the beginning with the Father: "And thou, Lord, in the beginning hast laid the foundation of the earth; and the heavens are the works of thine hands." Genesis 1:1 supports this, since the word "God" used in that verse is a uni-plural noun.

After Jesus had been baptized by John the Baptist, as he went up out of the water, a voice came from heaven, saying, "This is my beloved Son, in whom I am well pleased" (Matthew 3:17).

5. *The Holy Spirit Assures Us He Is God.* The Bible, which is inspired by the Holy Spirit, is the witness of the Spirit in assuring us that Christ is God.

In Mark 12:35-36 Jesus himself refers to the words of David as inspired by the Holy Spirit: ". . . How say the scribes that Christ is the son of David? For David himself said by the Holy Ghost, The Lord saith to my Lord, Sit thou on my right hand, till I make thine enemies thy footstool."

Paul, writing in I Corinthians 12:3, declares that men can confess the deity of Christ only by the Holy Spirit: ". . . No man speaking by the Spirit of God calleth Jesus accursed; and that no man can say that Jesus is the Lord, but by the Holy Ghost."

6. *Jesus Himself Avers That He Is God.* In John 10:30 he says, "I and the Father are one." Speaking to the Jews in John 5:17-23, he declares that he and the Father are one. Whatever is done in the matter of miracles, judgment, and the raising of the dead is done through both the Father and the Son, and "He that honoreth not the Son honoreth not the Father which hath sent him" (5:23).

Jesus, through his life on earth, climaxed by his death and glorious resurrection, fulfilled everything the New Testament said concerning his deity.

7. *The New Testament Asserts That He Is God.* "In the beginning was the Word, and the Word was with God, and the Word was God" (John 1:1). ". . . concerning his Son Jesus Christ our Lord . . . declared to be the Son of God with power, according to the spirit of holiness, by the resurrection from the dead" (Romans 1:3-4). "For in him dwelleth all the fulness of the Godhead bodily" (Colossians 2:9).

8. *Myriad Multitudes Avow Him To Be God.* Thomas called him God (Matthew 20:28), and Jesus did not rebuke him for this; rather he commended Thomas, and commends all those who would make the same acknowledgement (Matthew 20:29).

When Peter and the others saw him walking on the sea, Peter asked that the Lord bid him come over the waves also. Jesus bade him come, and Peter walked on the water until he became afraid; then he began to sink and cried out, "Lord, save me." Jesus stretched out his hand and caught him (Matthew 14:25-31). When they came into the ship, the winds ceased. "Then they that were in the ship came and worshipped him, saying, Of a truth thou art the Son of God" (Matthew 14:32-33).

When Jesus came to the grave of Lazarus, he asked Martha if she believed he was the resurrection and the life. She replied, "Yea, Lord; I believe that thou art the Christ, the Son of God, which should come into the world" (John 11:27).

Ananias, when he was sent to Paul, told him that "the Lord,

even Jesus" had sent him that Paul might receive his sight, "and be filled with the Holy Ghost" (Acts 9:17).

Modern man also attests to Christ's divinity. Philips Brooks said of Jesus: "I am far within the mark when I say that all the armies that ever marched, and all the navies that ever were built, and all the parliaments that ever sat, and all the kings that ever reigned, put together, have not affected the life of man upon this earth as powerfully as has that one solitary life—the life of Christ."

D. J. Burrell tells of two non-believers who were discussing the wonderful life of Jesus. "I think an interesting romance could be written about him," one declared. Then the other replied, "And you are just the man to write it. Set forth the prevailing sentiment as to his divinity and paint him as he was —a man among men."

The suggestion was followed and the romance was written. The man who suggested it was Colonel Ingersoll, the author was General Lew Wallace, and the book was *Ben Hur*. As he studied Christ's life in preparation for writing the book, he came to the profound conviction that Jesus was more than just a man among men. Before he had finished his book he had cried, "This was the Son of God!"

Some years ago two missionaries entered a town in Poland and challenged the local rabbi to a public debate on whether Jesus was the Christ. The discussion continued for three days, and finally the missionaries were cast out, spat upon, and beaten. They barely escaped with their lives.

The rabbi was acclaimed as the hero of truth. On the next sabbath, however, he did not conduct the service, nor did he appear the following sabbath. Finally on the third sabbath he sent word that it was urgent that he speak to his entire congregation. Very pale, he arose and spoke solemnly: "You all are aware of the recent controversy. You were good enough to acclaim me as victor in that debate. As I have to stand before the Judge of all the earth, I must tell you, let the apparent consequences be what they may, that *I* was conquered; and I am here to say that Jesus of Nazareth is the Messiah of whom Moses and the law spoke."

Someone has said of him:

> "His birth was contrary to the laws of life. His death was contrary to the laws of death. He had no cornfields or fisheries, but he could spread a table for five thousand and have bread and fish to spare. He walked on no beautiful carpets or velvet rugs, but he walked on the waters of the Sea of Galilee and they supported him. Three years he preached his gospel. He wrote no book, built no church house, had no monetary backing, but after nineteen hundred years he is the central character of human history, the pivot around which the ages revolve, and the only regenerator of the human race."

Another said of him:

> Socrates taught for forty years, Plato for fifty, Aristotle for forty, and Jesus for only three; yet those three years infinitely transcend in influence the combined one hundred and thirty years of teaching of the three greatest men of antiquity.
>
> Jesus painted no pictures; yet the paintings of Raphael, Michelangelo, and Leonardo da Vinci received their inspiration from him. Jesus wrote no poetry; but Dante, Milton, and scores of the world's greatest poets were inspired by him. Jesus composed no music; still Haydn, Handel, Beethoven, Bach, and Mendelssohn reached their highest perfection of melody in the hymns, symphonies, and oratorios written in his praise.

But Jesus is more than just another great teacher. He not only set the example because he was very God, righteous and holy, but he also gives the power of God to all those who are born again by his Spirit.

I served as pastor in a small Virginia town which had its "town drunk." He had once been a successful business man, highly respected and well liked. But liquor had taken its toll on him. His teen-age son and daughter were so embarrassed by his escapades that they withdrew themselves almost completely from the normal social life which young people enjoy. His wife, prematurely gray, was forced to seek employment in order to meet the needs of the family.

I visited him one day when he was confined to his bed, suffering from the after-effects of several days of drinking. "I want to tell you of Jesus, who can save you from this terrible thing," I said to him.

"Oh, I wish he could help me," he cried; "but now I am beyond all help. I have no power to withstand temptation."

"No one is beyond his help," I persisted; and then I read several Bible passages to him and prayed with him and for him. These actions were repeated over a period of several weeks until finally, during special evangelistic services, he came forward at the invitation to receive Christ. Kneeling, he began to pour out his woes to God.

"Oh, God, have mercy upon me," he pleaded. "I don't see how you could ever forgive a miserable wretch like me; but, Lord, I'm at the end of the way unless you save me and help me to overcome this awful craving which is mine."

God heard his plea; and he went away with assurance in his heart that Christ had saved him and would give him the power which he desperately needed.

Many years have gone since then, and Christ has marvelously used this man to influence others to accept him.

9. *The Whole Universe Shall Acclaim Him As God.* John, in the gospel, declares that the Father has sent the Son that he may receive the same honor which is given to God (5:23). John also predicts in Revelation that every creature in heaven, on the earth, and under the earth, and in the sea shall honor, bless, and glorify him forever and ever (5:13).

Paul declares in Philippians 2:10-11: "That at the name of Jesus every knee should bow, of things in heaven, and things in the earth, and things under the earth; and that every tongue should confess that Jesus Christ is Lord, to the glory of God the Father."

A group of prominent literary figures, meeting in London many years ago, were discussing great men of the past.

One of the men asked, "Gentlemen, what would you do if Milton entered this room?"

Another quickly replied, "We would give him such an ovation as might compensate for the tardy recognition accorded him by the men of his own day."

"And if Shakespeare entered?" asked another.

"We would arise and crown him master of song," decided another.

"And if Jesus Christ were to enter?"

"I think," said Charles Lamb amid a great silence, "we would all fall on our faces."

The whole universe some day will acclaim him as King of kings and Lord of lords.

CHAPTER THREE

Resurrection: "He Lives on High"

"... The Lord is risen indeed ..." (Lk. 24:34).

SEVERAL YEARS AGO a well-known ecclesiastic of the day startled adherents of evangelical Christianity with this pronouncement: "As far as I am concerned the dust of Christ's body still rests in a Syrian tomb. Whether or not he arose from the dead makes little difference to my faith."

The so-called social gospel does not always deny such a vital truth, but it often grossly neglects the event and doctrine of the resurrection and other events and doctrines of the Bible.

Dr. W. A. Criswell has this to say about some present-day social preaching:

> The emphasis in most of the culturally accepted preaching of modernity has been impersonal. It has stressed social ills rather than personal sin. The great themes of the modern pulpit have been those centering in social and economic justice: the saving of democracy, the national ills of the world, pacifism and the crusade for peace. If they were not preaching world peace, then the clergy were occupied with race discrimination, international relationships, the promotion of cultural and fraternal movements, the necessity for civic improvements, the furthering of international justice. Having lost faith in the scriptures, and with hearts that were spiritually empty, they found in these social subjects themes for their sermons.[1]

Not only was Christ's resurrection prophesied, predicted, and accomplished, but it is of vital importance to one's faith, the aforementioned ecclesiastic notwithstanding. Paul cries in

[1] W. A. Criswell, *These Issues We Must Face*, p. 21.

31

clarion tones: "That if thou shalt confess with thy mouth the
Lord Jesus, and shalt believe in thine heart that God raised him
from the dead, thou shalt be saved. For with the heart man believeth unto righteousness; and with the mouth confession is
made unto salvation" (Romans 10:9-10). Where there is no
hope in his resurrection, there is no hope in a resurrection for
one who may claim to be a believer in Christ.

The resurrection of Christ became the predominant theme
in the message of the early church. After the betrayal by Judas,
Peter in Acts 1 declared that another must be chosen "to be a
witness with us of the resurrection" (Acts 1:22). In Acts 4,
when the apostles had prayed, they were empowered by the
Holy Ghost, "and with great power gave witness of the resurrection of the Lord Jesus; and great grace was upon them all"
(Acts 4:33). The burden of Paul's message was Christ's death
and resurrection (Acts 17:2-3, 18).

Christ arose from the dead, for the Old Testament *prophesied*
it; Christ himself *predicted* it; the New Testament *portrays* it;
the empty tomb *prescribes* it; the transformation of the disciples
proves it; and the experience of believers *points* to it.

I. *THE OLD TESTAMENT PROPHESIED HIS RESUR-RECTION*

1. *It was foretold in direct prophecy.* "Therefore my heart
is glad, and my glory rejoiceth; my flesh also shall rest in hope.
For thou wilt not leave my soul in hell; neither wilt thou suffer
thine Holy One to see corruption" (Psalm 16:9-10). Peter,
preaching on that great day of Pentecost, filled with the Holy
Ghost, shows us that David is speaking about Christ in this
Psalm. He says, "For David speaketh concerning him, I fore-
saw the Lord always before my face, for he is on my right hand,
that I should not be moved. Therefore did my heart rejoice, and
my tongue was glad; moreover also my flesh shall rest in
hope; because thou wilt not leave my soul in hell, neither wilt
thou suffer thine Holy One to see corruption" (Acts 2:25-27).

Isaiah 53:10, Psalm 22:21 and John 20:17 should also be studied
as examples of Old Testament prophecy concerning his resurrection.

2. *His resurrection is pictured in types.* Isaac, in Genesis 22:2-13, not only pictures the death of Jesus, but also his ultimate resurrection. Hebrews 11:17-19 refers to this: "By faith Abraham when he was tried, offered up his only begotten son, of whom it was said, That in Isaac shall thy seed be called; accounting that God was able to raise him up, even from the dead; from whence also he received him in a figure."

Jonah is also a type of Christ, and his resurrection. His being swallowed by the fish, his soul descending into Sheol, from which he cried, and his later being vomited from the fish, all typify the death, burial and resurrection of Christ (Jonah 1:17-2:7). Christ later confirms this, for in Matthew 12:40 he says, "For as Jonas was three days and three nights in the whale's belly; so shall the Son of man be three days and three nights in the heart of the earth."

A traveler in Switzerland, uncertain of his way, asked a boy where Kaudersteg was, and received this reply: "I do not know where Kaudersteg is, but there is the road to it." And he pointed to the road ahead. We may not know the exact location of heaven, but we have been shown the way: God points out plainly the road to heaven as he reveals the resurrection of Christ, even in the Old Testament.

II. *CHRIST HIMSELF PREDICTED IT*

"Jesus said unto them, Destroy this temple, and in three days I will raise it up. Then said the Jews, Forty and six years was this temple in building, and wilt thou rear it up in three days? But he spake of the temple of his body. When therefore he was risen from the dead, his disciples remembered that he had said this unto them; and they believed the scripture, and the word which Jesus had said" (John 2:19-22).

Jesus also refers to the fact of his resurrection in John 10:17-18: "Therefore doth my Father love me, because I lay down my life, that I might take it again. No man taketh it from me, but I lay it down of myself. I have power to lay it down, and I have power to take it again. This commandment have I received of my Father."

In these and other passages Jesus taught his disciples that he was to die, and be raised again the third day (Matthew 16:21;17: 22-23; 20:18-19).

A mother took her small child to a dangerous spot of the sea and gently led him into the edge of the water. When the ripples of water wet his feet he clung to her in fear. But with gentle words and affectionate caresses she led him there again and again. At length he lost his fear and toddled alone while his mother watched. When a passerby inquired as to what she was doing, she replied, "I am drawing out his fear." Christ leads his followers to the very brink of the abyss and points to them the hope of the resurrection!

III. *THE NEW TESTAMENT PORTRAYS THE RESURRECTION*

1. *It is recorded as a historical fact.* We are told that there are "many infallible proofs." "To whom also he showed himself alive after his passion by many infallible proofs, being seen of them forty days, and speaking of the things pertaining to the kingdom of God" (Acts 1:3).

Peter, speaking on the day of Pentecost, declares, "This Jesus hath God raised up, whereof we all are witnesses" (Acts 2: 32). Again, after the conversion of Cornelius, he declares, "And we are witnesses of all things which he did both in the land of the Jews, and in Jerusalem; whom they slew and hanged on a tree; him God raised up the third day, and showed him openly; not to all the people, but unto witnesses chosen before of God, even to us, who did eat and drink with him after he rose from the dead" (Acts 10:39-41).

Paul affirms in I Corinthians 15:3-8 that Christ was seen after his resurrection, first by Cephas, then of the twelve, and following these he was seen by more than five hundred brethren. He then showed himself to James, and again to the twelve. Finally, the apostle declares, "And last of all he was seen of me also, as of one born out of due time" (15:8).

2. *It is the basis of Christian doctrine.* Paul says Jesus is "declared to be the Son of God with power . . . by the resurrection from the dead" (Romans 1:4). Again, he declares in Romans 4:25, "[He] was raised again for our justification." The doc-

trines of baptism, and holiness in the life of a Christian are based on the fact of Christ's resurrection (Romans 6:4, 8-12; Colossians 3:1). And, most importantly, our own hope for resurrection is based on Christ's resurrection (II Corinthians 4:14).

We see then that the doctrines of Christ's deity, justification, baptism, holiness, and the believer's resurrection are all based on Christ's resurrection. In fact, the entire structure of Christian teaching rests upon the certainty that Christ arose; for Paul tells us in I Corinthians 15:14 that "If Christ be not risen, then is our preaching vain, and your faith is also vain."

Dr. Wilbur M. Smith says of the great fact of resurrection:

> Whatever be one's final conviction regarding the resurrection of our Lord, it is admitted by everyone that such a supposed event is so interwoven with all the New Testament documents that to eliminate it from the gospels, the Acts, and the epistles, is to render the entire New Testament record hopelessly confused. It would be to deny not only certain words of our Lord in his teaching, but also to repudiate many accusations made against him by his enemies; it would be to make the end of our Lord's life nothing but a tragedy.[1]

Before Columbus discovered America, Spain's coat of arms bore the motto, *Ne Plus Ultra* — "There is nothing beyond." After Columbus' discovery, the *Ne* was dropped from the coat of arms, leaving *Plus Ultra* — "There is more beyond."

Before Jesus came into the world, there were many who thought: "There is nothing beyond." They died in the depths of despair. But after Jesus' death on the cross and resurrection from the dead, people everywhere could joyously cry, "There is more beyond! Christ is risen, and he lives! Because he lives we can live also!"

IV. THE EMPTY TOMB PRESCRIBES IT

There is no doubt that the tomb was empty. The women and those with them came to the tomb very early in the morning on the first day of the week and they found the stone rolled away from the sepulchre. When they entered the tomb, they found that it was empty (Luke 24:13; John 20:1-9).

[1] Wilbur M. Smith, *The Supernaturalness of Christ,* p. 193.

Mary wept sorely when she came to the tomb and found
that the Lord was not there. But how we would all still be
weeping if he had still been buried there! He would be no
Saviour. If Mary had only remembered the words of her Lord
that he would rise again, she would have shouted with joy when
she found the tomb empty.

> "Mary!" just one word;
> 'Twas all he need employ
> To turn a woman's sorrowing heart
> Into a well of joy.

The question naturally arises, What became of his body?

His enemies did not take it, for they would have produced
it in order to disprove the story of the resurrection.

His friends did not steal it, for they would not later have
suffered for what they knew to be false.

There is, then, but one satisfactory explanation of the empty
tomb—Christ arose!

A father and son were shipwrecked. Together they clung to
the wreckage until finally the son disappeared from sight. Later,
unconscious, the father was rescued. When he awoke he learned
that he was in a fisherman's hut. His thoughts immediately
turned to his boy. But then as he turned he saw that his boy
was lying alive beside him. The tempests of life will soon engulf
us and we shall be swept away, but in Christ we shall all be together again. Because he lives, we shall live also!

The fact that the tomb was empty proves that the resurrection of Christ was a *physical* resurrection. The body which
was crucified rose from the dead. His *flesh* did not see corruption (Acts 2:31).

Two boys were slaves to an Arab master. He taught them to
believe in Mohammed, whose body, they were told, was preserved in the city of Medina. One day the lads heard a missionary tell about the death, burial and resurrection of Jesus.
That night they talked about what they had heard. "What think
you?" said one. "Our master tells us to believe in Mohammed,
who is dead; but the white man tells us to believe in Jesus,
who died but rose again and is now alive." After a moment the
other said, "I think I will believe in the Living One." After

their acceptance of Christ as Saviour they were taken to the
mission station where they were taught by the missionary.

V. THE TRANSFORMATION OF THE DISCIPLES PROVES THE RESURRECTION

1. *Deserters became bold.* Peter is a classic example. While
Christ was being tried he not only deserted his Lord but denied
him three times (Mark 14:66-72). Notice the transformation,
however, which had come over Peter when he preached his
immortal sermon on the day of Pentecost. "This Jesus hath God
raised up, whereof we are all witnesses" (Acts 2:14, 23, 32).

2. *Doubters were convinced.* Thomas, who was absent when
the Lord first appeared to the disciples after his resurrection,
refused to believe when they later recounted their meeting with
Christ. Eight days later the Lord again appeared to the disciples
and this time Thomas was with them. When Thomas beheld
him he exclaimed, "My Lord and my God" (John 20:24-29).

The Marquess of Salisbury once avowed: "To me, the central
point is the resurrection of Christ, which I believe. First, because it is testified by men who had every opportunity of seeing
and knowing, and whose veracity was tested by the most tre-
mendous trials, both of energy and endurance. Secondly, because of the marvelous effect it had on the world. As a moral
phenomenon, the spread and mastery of Christianity is without a parallel. I can no more believe that colossal moral effects
lasting for two thousand years can be without a cause
than I can believe that the various motions of the magnet are
without a cause, though I cannot wholly explain them. To anyone who believes the resurrection of Christ, the rest presents
little difficulty. No one who has that belief will doubt that
those who were commissioned by him to speak carried a divine
message."

3. *Discouragement was changed to assurance.* Cleopas and
his friend were sad on that first day of the week as they
journeyed towards Emmaus. Their hopes and dreams were all
shattered—or so they thought. When Jesus came and walked
with them, they at first did not recognize him. Later, as he sat
at bread with them, their eyes were opened and they knew him

as the resurrected Lord. They were filled with assurance as they hurried to tell the others the things which had come to pass (Luke 24:17, 21, 31-35).

4. *Disbelievers were converted.* Paul, as he witnessed to King Agrippa, recounted his own conversion, how the resurrected Christ spoke to him from heaven after he was struck down on the road to Damascus. Prior to that time, this Pharisee had refused to recognize the Messiah, but since that time he was converted, for he knew that the crucified Jesus is the living Christ! (Acts 26:8-23).

VI. *THE EXPERIENCE OF BELIEVERS POINTS TO IT*

We know Christ lives because he lives in us. We can say with Paul, "I am crucified with Christ; nevertheless I live; yet not I, but Christ liveth in me; and the life which I now live in the flesh I live by the faith of the Son of God, who loved me, and gave himself for me" (Galatians 2:20) .

Dr. Reichel was conducting his choir in final rehearsal before presenting the *Messiah*. The chorus had sung to the point where the soprano soloist takes up the refrain, "I know that my Redeemer liveth." The soloist's technique was perfect. When she had finished, all eyes were on Reichel, expecting his look of approval.

After he had silenced the orchestra he came to the side of the soloist, and with sorrowful expression he said, "My daughter, do you really know that your Redeemer liveth?" She blushed as she faltered, "Why, yes, I think I do."

"Then sing it!" cried the master. "Tell it to me so that I will know and all who hear you will know the joy and power of it."

She then sang the truth as she knew it and had experienced it in her own heart, and all who heard wept as she sang.

When she had finished the great musician approached her with tear-filled eyes and declared, "You do know, for you have told me."

We know Christ lives, for we have received the life of his resurrection. "Knowing that Christ being raised from the dead dieth no more; death hath no more dominion over him. Likewise reckon ye also yourselves to be dead indeed unto sin, but alive unto God through Jesus Christ our Lord" (Romans 6:9, 11).

Finally, we know Christ lives because we commune with the *living Christ*. "If ye then be risen with Christ, seek those things which are above, where Christ sitteth on the right hand of God" (Colossians 3:1). "That which we have seen and heard declare we unto you, that ye may also have fellowship with us; and truly our fellowship is with the Father, and with his Son Jesus Christ" (I John 1:3).

A little lad, stricken with a fatal malady, called his doctor into his room and said, "Doctor, I want you to get me well by Sunday."

"Why by Sunday?" asked the doctor kindly.

"Well, our teacher showed us the tabernacle last Sunday. We saw the outside, but there was a curtain and we could not see inside. Teacher said the priest went in behind the curtain to talk with God, and she is going to show us the place next Sunday. Oh, doctor, I hope I can go; I do so want to see inside where God is."

The doctor turned from the window where he had been standing, and placed his large hand on the little one. "Next Sunday, Charles, you may see the place where God is."

Next Sunday he had gone from earth to "the place where God is."

We may all have that same assurance through the promises of the resurrected Christ!

CHAPTER FOUR

Grace: "Greater Than All My Sins"

"For by grace are ye saved through faith; and that not
of yourselves; it is the gift of God" (Ephesians 2:8).

DURING THE SPANISH-AMERICAN WAR Colonel Theodore Roose-
velt sought to purchase from the Red Cross some delicacies for
his men. When he was told that he could not buy them, he
inquired, "How can I get these things?" He was told, "Just ask
for them, Colonel." So it is with grace. It cannot be bought,
but it can be sought and it can be secured—only as a free gift!

Relating the grace of God, someone has expressed it this
way: "Wonderful love that *thought* it; wonderful birth that
brought it; wonderful death that *wrought* it; and wonderful word
that *taught* it."

In order to study this blessed doctrine acceptably, we shall
discuss in this message the following: the *meaning* of grace; the
marvel of grace; the *marks* of grace; the *mastery* of grace; and
the *maturity* of grace.

I. THE MEANING OF GRACE

To understand more fully its meaning (no finite mind can
comprehend completely this wonderful bestowal of God!),
let us attempt to define it, contrast it, and note its source.

Grace is the attitude of God toward us in Christ. "For the
grace of God that bringeth salvation hath appeared to all men"
(Titus 2:11); grace is "the kindness and love of God our Saviour
toward men appeared" (Titus 3:4). Webster tells us that grace

40

is "unmerited favor." Eddleman says it is more than this: "It is sovereign love asserting itself against human apathy."

Grace is also this character or attitude of God reproduced in the believer. This may be called "imparted grace." We are told by Paul to teach, admonish, sing, and speak with "grace in your hearts" (Colossians 3:16; 4:6).

We need, also, to understand the meaning of grace by contrasting it with law. The law was given by Moses, "but grace and truth came by Jesus Christ" (John 1:17). Paul declares that the law reminds us of sin, but "sin shall not have dominion over you; for ye are not under the law, but under grace" (Romans 6:14). The grace of God through Christ offers us this undeserved favor to such an extent that God's just demands of judgment under the law are fully satisfied. "Law blesses the good; grace saves the bad. Law demands that blessings be earned; grace is a free gift."

Grace also should be contrasted with works. "By grace are ye saved through faith and that not of works" (Ephesians 2:8-9). "And if by grace, then is it no more of works; otherwise grace is no more grace" (Romans 11:6).

Dr. Chafer reminds us that grace cannot incur a debt:

> An act is in no sense gracious if under any conditions a debt is incurred. Grace, being unrecompensed favor, is necessarily unrecompensed as to obligations which are past, unrecompensed as to obligations which are present, and unrecompensed as to obligations which are future. Grace must always remain unadulterated in its generosity and benefit. How emphatically this is true of the grace of God towards sinners! Yet how often this aspect of divine salvation is perverted! Infinite and eternal transformations are wrought by the power of God when he exercises his grace. He is thereby glorified and sinners are saved. Such far-reaching results cannot fail to satisfy and delight him eternally; but he remains *unrecompensed* for his salvation through grace. What he does he bestows as a *gift*.[1]

The eminent evangelist Angel Martinez has declared:

> If you could carry human goodness to infinity, you could not earn one fraction of a percent of salvation. If we could gather every good man that ever lived in the history of the world, and

---

[1] Lewis Sperry Chafer, *Grace*, p. 6.

take from each one the best in his character, and combine these multiple qualities in one individual, that individual would still have to kneel at the cross and say, "Lord, be merciful to me a sinner."[2]

No less than 115 passages in the Bible tell us that grace depends only on *believing*; there are some 35 passages which declare that grace depends on *faith*, which is but a synonym of believing. Therefore, this grace cannot come through any work performed by man. In spite of this, however, there are those who contend that baptism is necessary to obtain this grace. Mark 16:16 is the only instance in the Bible where these two appear to be linked together as conditions for salvation. This is an appearance only, however, for the word *baptized* is absent from the negative statement, "he that believeth not shall be damned." This is evidence that baptism, which is administered by man, is not an essential condition in the positive statement.

Summing it up, then, we realize that this grace has its source in God the Father: "Grace . . . from God our Father and the Lord Jesus Christ" (Philemon 3); ". . . the God of all grace" (I Peter 5:10). Christ the Son is seen to be the author of grace as well, for II Corinthians 8:9 speaks of ". . . the grace of our Lord Jesus Christ." The Holy Spirit also has a wonderful part in this matchless gift, for Hebrews 10:29 refers to "the Spirit of grace."

There is an old story which tells of a mother who lay dying. Her parched lips thirsted for something to refresh them. By her bedside stood her fourteen-year-old daughter. Suddenly the thought struck her: "I have seen such beautiful grapes in the hothouses of the court gardens; I'll go and ask how much one bunch would be. Oh! if I could just get one bunch for mother!"

She slipped away with all haste and soon reached the court gardens. The sentry on guard asked her errand. "I must see the king," said the little maid. "Impossible!" replied the stern soldier. "But my mother is dying," she pleaded. "I can let no one pass these gates," was the reply. The poor child's heart sank, and she burst into tears.

2 Angel Martinez, *Crying in the Chapel,* p. 19.

Just at that moment the king's son rode up, and touched with the child's grief, inquired the cause; turning to her he said, "Well, and what do *you* want with the king?"

"Please, sir, mother's dying, and I want to know what is the price of grapes? Mother's so thirsty." And the tears flowed faster.

Bidding her follow him, the prince led her to one of the vines, and cutting with his own hands a fine bunch of the rich fruit, he gave it to the astonished child, saying, "My father does not sell—he gives." So the Heavenly Father, through his Son, gives a much greater gift to us.

II. *THE MARVEL OF GRACE*

What a wonderful thing God has done in providing the riches of his grace to all who will accept it!

Grace is *rich*. The Bible tells us that we have the riches of grace which provides redemption through Christ's blood and the forgiveness of sins (Ephesians 1:7). We are reminded that we shall be shown the riches of his grace in his kindness toward us (Ephesians 2:7). Recently, a famous television star, whose salary is in excess of $5,000 weekly, was led to accept Christ. In giving his testimony later he declared, "With all my income and wealth of material things, I came to realize that I was a pauper. Now, in Christ, I am rich because of his wonderful grace!"

Grace is *abundant*. "For if by one man's offense death reigned by one; much more they which receive abundance of grace and of the gift of righteousness shall reign in life by one, Jesus Christ. But where sin abounded, grace did much more abound" (Romans 5:17, 20).

Several years ago, in one of our large cities, there was a notorious night club where such sins as gambling, drinking, and adultery were purportedly practiced. Ultimately, the club was closed; and some months afterward the building was bought by a group of Christians who remodeled it and used it as a house of worship. They placed a huge sign over the main entrance to the building which read, "Where sin abounded, grace did much more abound."

Grace is *manifold*. "As every man hath received the gift, even so minister the same one to another, as good stewards of the manifold grace of God" (1 Peter 4:10).

Grace is *sufficient*. "My grace is sufficient for thee; for my grace is made perfect in weakness" (II Corinthians 12:9).

Grace is *sure*. "Therefore it is of faith, that it might be by grace; to the end the promise might be sure" (Romans 4:16).

Longfellow could take a worthless sheet of paper, write a poem on it, and make it worth $6,000—*that's genius.*

Rockefeller could sign his name to a piece of paper and make it worth a million dollars—*that's capital.*

Uncle Sam can take gold, stamp an eagle on it, and make it worth $20.00—*that's money.*

A craftsman can take material that is worth only $5.00 and made it worth $50.00—*that's skill.*

An artist can take an inexpensive piece of canvas, paint a picture on it, and make it worth $1,000—*that's art.*

God can take a worthless, sinful life, wash it in the blood of Christ, put his Spirit in it, and make it a blessing to humanity—*that's grace.*

Marvelous, wonderful grace! Who can plumb its depths? or who can ascend its heights? or who can fully comprehend its vast meaning? It is something which only God can provide and give!

III. *THE MARKS OF GRACE*

The Bible is emphatic as to the marks of grace. Of the man who has partaken of God's grace it is said that he is:

Selected by God (I Thessalonians 1:4; 5:24).

Saved through the blood of Christ (Colossians 1:14). Every sin is forgiven.

Sheltered eternally under the propitiation made in the blood of Christ (I John 2:2).

Sanctified positionally, or set apart unto God in Christ (I Corinthians 1:30).

Steadfast forever (Hebrews 10:14). "For by one offering he hath perfected forever them that are sanctified."

Sinless—made the righteousness of God in him (II Corinthians 5:21).

Separated from the law (Romans 7:4, 6). Being delivered from the law, he is dead to the law.

Safe from the power of darkness (Colossians 1:13). Deliverance *from* and translation *into* are noted here.

Surely founded on the Rock Christ Jesus (I Corinthians 3:11).

Supported by Christ's intercession (Hebrews 7:25).

Seated in the heavenly in Christ (Ephesians 2:6).

Stranger to earth, citizen of heaven (Philippians 3:20).

Sealed by the Spirit (Ephesians 4:30).

Surrounded by every spiritual blessing (Ephesians 1:3). This is the sphere of the believer's spiritual experience as identified with Christ in nature, life, relationships, service, suffering, inheritance, and future glory.

> He giveth more grace when the burdens grow greater.
> He sendeth more strength when the labors increase.
> To added affliction he addeth his mercy,
> To multiplied trials, his multiplied peace.
>
> When we have exhausted our store of endurance,
> When our strength has failed ere the day is half done,
> When we reach the end of our hoarded resources,
> Our Father's full giving has only begun.
>
> His love has no limits, his grace has no measure,
> ` His power no boundary known unto men.
> For out of his infinite riches in Jesus,
> He giveth, and giveth, and giveth, again.
>
> —J. E. Myhill

IV. *THE MASTERY OF GRACE*

We are delivered from the power of sin through this grace which comes into our lives by union with Christ. "How shall we that are dead to sin, live any longer therein?" (Romans 6:2). When the child of God remembers that he is no longer under the law but under grace (Romans 6:14), he will, through the inworking of the Holy Spirit, strive to master the Christian graces which are manifest in the fruits of the Spirit.

This Christian life will be supplemented constantly by the

wonderful grace of Christ, for we are *established* with grace;
we *grow* in grace; we *live* by grace; and our *consolation* and
eternal hope are through grace.

First, we are *established* with grace. "Be not carried about by
divers and strange doctrines. For it is a good thing that the
heart is established with grace" (Hebrews 13:9). The grace of
Christ will teach our hearts concerning doctrines, to know
whether they be of God or of man. We shall, through grace,
know the truth. In a day when men are taking away from God's
word, others are adding to it, and yet others are denying it,
we should be fully established in grace.

Second, we *grow* in grace. Paul declares in I Corinthians
that many were babes in Christ because they had not grown in
grace. The man who has reached a degree of spiritual maturity
has shown evidences of growth in grace through his life. This
is what Peter means when he exhorts: "But grow in grace, and
in the knowledge of our Lord and Saviour Jesus Christ" (II Peter
3:18). A bud may be perfect; but, if instead of developing into
a blossom, it remains a bud, its apparent perfection is the cover-
ing of a terrible deformity. Dr. W. H. Griffith Thomas has
said, "The Christian life is like riding a bicycle: if you do not
go on you go off."

Third, we *live* by grace. "For the grace of God . . . hath
appeared to all men, teaching us that, denying ungodliness and
worldly lusts, we should live soberly, righteously, and godly, in
this present world" (Titus 2:11-12).

D. L. Moody once declared:

> "A man can no more take a supply of grace for the future than
> he can eat enough today to last him for the next six months, or
> take sufficient air into his lungs to sustain life for a week to
> come. We must draw upon God's boundless stores for grace
> from day to day, as we need it."

Fourth, our *consolation* and *eternal hope* are through grace.
"Now our Lord Jesus Christ himself, and God, even our Father,
which hath loved us, and hath given us everlasting consolation
and good hope through grace, comfort your hearts, and stablish
you in every good word and work" (II Thessalonians 2:16-17).

Booth-Tucker preached in Chicago one day, and out from the throng a burdened toiler came and said to him, before all the audience, "You can talk like that about how Christ is dear to you, and helps you; but if your wife was dead, as my wife is, and you had babies crying for their mother who would never come back, you could not say what you are saying."

A little later Booth-Tucker lost his noble wife in a railroad accident, and her body was brought to Chicago and carried to the Salvation Army barracks for the funeral service. He looked down into the face of the silent wife and mother, and said, "The other day when I was here, a man said that I could not say Christ was sufficient if my wife were dead and my children were crying for their mother. If that man is here, tell him that Christ *is* sufficient. My heart is all broken, my heart is all crushed, my heart is all bleeding, but there is a song in my heart and Christ put it there; and if that man is here, I tell him that, though my wife is gone and my children are motherless, Christ comforts me today."

That man was there, and he came down the aisle and kneeled beside the casket, and said, "Verily, if Christ can help us like that, I will surrender to him."

V. *THE MATURITY OF GRACE*

What does the Bible tell us concerning grace and future glory? Grace is to be brought to us at the revelation of Christ. Then it is that the power and love of God shall be manifested (I Peter 1:13). Paul declares in Titus 2:11-13 that the grace of God, which has appeared to all men, causes us to look for the blessed hope and the glorious appearing of Christ. Again, the great apostle refreshes our spirits by reminding us that the grace of Christ caused our Lord to become poor in order that we may become rich (II Corinthians 8:9). This will all culminate in Christ's return when our faith becomes sight. "That in the ages to come he might show the exceeding riches of his grace in his kindness toward us through Christ Jesus" (Ephesians 2:7). The grace of God, then, will become complete at Christ's second advent. We should look forward to that great event with anticipation. To anticipate with love his appearing will produce in us seven things:

Prudent watchfulness. "Watch ye therefore . . . I say unto you all, Watch" (Mark 13:35, 37).

Persistent abiding in him. "And now, little children, abide in him; that, when he shall appear, we may have confidence, and not be ashamed before him at his coming" (I John 2:28).

Purposeful right living. "Let your moderation be known to all men. The Lord is at hand" (Philippians 4:5).

Purity in our lives. "Beloved, now are we the sons of God, and it doth not yet appear what we shall be; but we know that, when he shall appear, we shall be like him; for we shall see him as he is. And every man that hath this hope in him purifieth himself, even as he is pure" (I John 3:2-3).

Peace and comfort in the heart. "Then we . . . shall be caught up to meet the Lord . . . wherefore comfort one another with these words (I Thessalonians 4:17-18).

Patience. "Be patient, therefore, brethren, unto the coming of the Lord" (James 5:7).

Profitable service. "I charge thee therefore before God, and the Lord Jesus Christ, who shall judge the quick and the dead at his appearing and his kingdom: Preach the word, be instant in season, out of season; reprove, rebuke, exhort with all longsuffering and doctrine" (II Timothy 4:1-2).

Kenneth Wuest has said, "The word *grace* is probably the greatest word in the New Testament, greater even than *love*, for grace is love in action, and therefore includes it." This is true, for the grace of God is the very foundation of all the wonderful promises of God's word.

A little boy, one of seven children, met with an accident, and was taken to the hospital. He came from a poor home where hunger was seldom completely satisfied. The glass of milk was only part full, or if full, shared by two of the children. After the lad was made comfortable in his hospital bed, a nurse brought him a large glass of milk. He looked at it longingly and then, with the memory of many experiences of sharing with the other children, said, "How deep shall I drink?" The nurse with her eyes shining and a lump in her throat said, "Drink it all." Oh, hungry and thirsty soul, how deep shall you drink of the love and goodness of God? There is no limit! Drink it all, drink it again and again! The supply is inexhaustible.

CHAPTER FIVE

Faith: *"Have Faith in God"*

> "Therefore being justified by faith, we have peace with God through our Lord Jesus Christ" (Rom. 5:1).

DURING A CONVERSATION with a fellow passenger on a train, Dr. A. J. Gordon gave testimony to his faith in Christ for the forgiveness of his sins. But the other objected. "I believe that when God receives one into heaven he makes a searching inquiry as to his character rather than inspection of his faith," he declared.

Soon the conductor came along to examine and receive the tickets. When he had gone, Dr. Gordon said: "Did you ever notice how a conductor looks at the ticket and takes no pains to inspect the passenger? A railway ticket, if genuine, certifies that the person presenting it has complied with the company's conditions and is entitled to transportation. So faith alone entitles one to that saving grace which produces a character well pleasing to God. 'Without faith it is impossible to please him.'"

Hebrews 11:1 informs us that "faith is the assurance of things hoped for, the proving of things not seen." Faith, then, "is a hope that is absolutely certain that what it believes is true, and that what it expects will come." This hope is something which looks forward with more than wishful longing; it views the future with complete certainty. Since faith is the evidence of things not seen, to discuss this subject fully becomes a mighty undertaking indeed. It will prove very worthwhile, however, to consider all ramifications of this wonderful doctrine. We must, of necessity, divide our study into two parts: (1) the *foundation* of faith, and (2) the *fruits* of faith.

I. *THE FOUNDATION OF FAITH.* We need to note here the *channel*, the *content*, the *caliber*, and the *cause* of faith.

1. *The Channel of Faith*—whom we believe. We are, first of all, to believe in God. "And Jesus answering saith unto them, Have faith in God" (Mark 11:22). "For what saith the scripture? Abraham believed God, and it was counted unto him for righteousness" (Romans 4:3). Paul declares in the record of Acts 27:25, "I believe God." And so should we. Jesus declares in John 5:24, "He that heareth my word, and believeth on him that sent me, hath everlasting life." He is referring here to God.

Two little children were once hired by a skeptic to carry through the neighborhood streets a sign which read, "God is nowhere." Somehow the words became separated so that the sign which they displayed read, "God is now here." God is real; he is the true God; he is the only God with whom we have to do. Let us hope in him; let us hear him; let us heed him.

Secondly, we are to believe in Christ as the only begotten Son of God. Jesus himself said, "Ye believe in God, believe also in me" (John 14:1). In Acts 16:31 we have the combined testimony of Paul and Silas, who declared, "Believe on the Lord Jesus Christ, and thou shalt be saved." It is then with this Jesus, the manifestation of God in the flesh, that we have to do. This naturally leads us to our consideration of faith's content.

2. *The Content of Faith*—what we believe. First, we must believe in *the deity of Christ.* "But these are written, that ye might believe that Jesus is the Christ, the Son of God. . ." (John 20:31). "And he said . . . I am from above . . . for if ye believe not that I am he, ye shall die in your sins" (John 8:23-24). "Whosoever believeth that Jesus is the Christ is born of God" (I John 5:1). See also John 16:27, 30; 17:8, 21.

Certainly he was God, this man who dwelt among us and who could think the thoughts of God; who could talk and through his words transport us to the presence of God himself; who could teach the truth of God to thrill the hearts of men; who testified to the transcending power of God which can be manifested in our lives through faith; who alone has the power to thwart the temptations of Satan and triumph over him. To such a man we must ascribe deity, and cry from the depths of our souls, "My Lord and my God!"

Second, we must believe in *the death of Christ* as the only means of atonement for our sins. For we are justified by his grace through the redemption that he has provided, he whom God has set forth as a propitiation through faith in his blood (Romans 3:24-25).

Paul said, "I am not ashamed of the gospel of Christ; for it is the power of God unto salvation to everyone that believeth" (Romans 1:16). "Moreover, brethren, I declare unto you the gospel . . . by which also ye are saved . . . how that Christ died for our sins" (I Corinthians 15:1-3).

Third, we must believe in *the deliverance of Christ* through resurrection. Romans 10:9 tells us that we must believe that God raised Christ from the dead; and Paul emphasizes that "if Christ be not risen, your faith is vain" (I Corinthians 15:17). "For us also . . . it shall be imputed, if we believe on him that raised up Jesus our Lord from the dead" (Romans 4:24).

Congress once issued a special edition of Jefferson's Bible. It was simply a copy of the Bible with all references to the supernatural deleted. Jefferson confined himself solely to the moral teachings of Jesus. The closing words to his Bible are: "There laid they Jesus, and rolled a great stone to the mouth of the sepulchre and departed." Thank God, the Bible does not really end like that! Our hope is in Christ's resurrection.

There is no saving faith aside from the belief in Christ's resurrection. This, then, becomes the very foundation of our faith, for without it falsehood would replace truth; evil would overcome good; hatred would displace love; and death would be stronger than life. "Take away the resurrection," says Paul, "and you destroy both the foundation and fabric of Christian faith."

The funeral service for Dr. F. B. Meyer in London was one of radiant joy. Scripture passages and hymns on the resurrection theme were heard. At the close of the service the congregation stood, fully expecting a funeral march, but instead the organist played the Halleluiah Chorus. That is the faith which is ours today! We worship a living Christ!

3. *The Caliber of Faith*—how we believe. There must, first of all, be faith *in the heart*. A mere mental acquiescence is not sufficient. The heart is spoken of as the seat of our emotions; and the intellect, the emotions and the will must all be exercised before saving faith can be manifested. "Believe in thine heart" (Romans 10:9-10). Here is the basis of faith. The Greek word for Lord is *kurios*. This is a key word here, for it implies that when one called Jesus *kurios*, he was giving him the supreme place in his life; he was giving him complete obedience and reverent worship; he was trusting him as God. More than this,—though he has not seen him nor did he witness the event— he must believe that Jesus has risen from the dead. He must believe that Christ not only *lived*, but still *lives*. He must not only know *about Christ*. He must *know Christ*.

Second, faith must be *unfeigned* (I Timothy 1:5). There must be sincerity and genuineness. No ulterior motives can enter here. Paul, in writing to Timothy, reminds him that his unfeigned faith bears great responsibility and brings many rewards (II Timothy 1:5-7). Because of such faith there is courage, power, love, and self-discipline.

Third, there is the *obedience of faith* (Romans 16:26). God's word demands submission; this is the exercise of faith. It is not an obedience founded on submission to an iron law, which breaks the man who opposes it; but rather it is an obedience founded on surrender as a result of love (Galatians 5:6). Abraham is a classic example of such obedience (Hebrews 11:8).

4. *The Cause of Faith*—how it is obtained. Faith is the *instrument* of God, the holy Trinity. "God hath dealt to every man the measure of faith" (Romans 12:3). Jesus is the author and finisher of our faith (Hebrews 12:2). "But the fruit of the Spirit is . . . faith" (Galatians 5:22).

Faith is *imparted* through the word. "Faith cometh by hearing and hearing by the word of God" (Romans 10:17). Peter and John preached the word and multitudes "of them which heard the word believed" (Acts 4::4). In the conclusion of his gospel John tells us that "these are written, that ye might believe that Jesus is the Christ, the Son of God; and that believing ye might have life through his name" (John 20:31). D. L. Moody said there was a time in his life when he spent much time in prayer seeking greater faith. He would often say, "What we want is faith; if we only have faith we can turn Chicago upside down, or rather right side up." He expected faith to strike him like lightning. However, it did not seem to come. One day he read Romans 10:17, and found the answer. "I closed my Bible and prayed for faith. Then I opened my Bible and began to study, and faith has been growing ever since."

Prayer is an ingredient of faith, for faith is *increased* in answer to prayer. "Lord, I believe; help thou mine unbelief" (Mark 9:24). "Increase our faith" (Luke 17:5). Jesus, in speaking to Simon, said, "I have prayed for thee, that thy faith fail not" (Luke 22:32).

II. *THE FRUITS OF FAITH.* These are *salvation, satisfaction, supplication,* and *service.*

1. *Faith and Salvation.* Here we must consider justification, regeneration, and sanctification.

We are *justified* by our faith (Romans 5:1; Galatians 2:16). Justification requires the removal of sin and guilt; the bestowal of righteousness. Justification and righteousness are inseparably united in scripture by the fact that the same word root is used for both: *dikaios,* "righteous"; *dikaioo,* "to justify." Sin and guilt are removed and righteousness is bestowed through faith, bringing justification. He that ". . . believeth, his faith is counted for righteousness" (Romans 4:5). Romans 3:22 and Acts 10:43 also speaks of the bestowal of righteousness.

We are *regenerated by* faith. "Whosoever believeth . . . is born of God" (I John 5:1). "For ye are all the children of God by faith in Christ Jesus" (Galatians 3:26). See also John 20:31.

To be regenerated one must exercise faith unto salvation. Nothing less will do. Bishop John Taylor Smith was preaching many years ago in a large cathedral. His subject was the new birth of the converted man. At one point he declared, "You might even be an arch-deacon like my friend here and not be born again." A day or so later he received a letter from the arch-deacon, in which he wrote: "You have found me out. I have been a clergyman for over thirty years, but I have never known Christian joy. Mine has been a hard, legal service." The bishop and the arch-deacon were later on their knees, the latter crying to God for mercy and salvation. He was soon born again.

We are *sanctified* by faith. ". . . that they may receive forgiveness of sins, and inheritance among them which are sanctified by faith that is in me" (Acts 26:18). The verb "sanctify" is used 133 times in both the Old and New Testaments. The noun "sanctification" is used six times, only in the New Testament. The basic meaning of the verb is "to separate" or to "set apart." The Holy Spirit, who comes into the believer's heart through faith, sanctifies him, sets him apart, for righteous, useful, fruitful living.

Bishop Ryle affirms this in his definition:

> Sanctification is the inward spiritual work which the Lord Jesus Christ works in a man by the Holy Ghost, when he calls him to be a true believer. He not only washed him from his sins in his own blood, but he also *separates* him from his natural love of sin and the world, puts a new principle in his heart, and makes him practically godly in life.[1]

We are, therefore, *saved* by faith. Ephesians 2:8 and Luke 7:50 confirms this. It has been said: "Trust in yourself, and you are doomed to disappointment; trust in your friends, and they will die and leave you; trust in money, and you may have it taken from you; trust in reputation, and some slanderous tongue may blast it; but trust in God, and you are never to be confounded in time or eternity."

2. *Faith and Satisfaction.* We have *assurance* through faith. "Whosoever believeth . . . shall not be ashamed" (Roman 10:11). "I know whom I have believed, and am persuaded that he is able to keep that which I have committed unto him against that day" (II Timothy 1:12). "Draw near . . . in full assurance of faith" (Hebrews 10:22). A Christian asked another how he was getting along. Dolefully his friend replied, "Oh, fairly well,

1 J. C. Ryle, *Holiness*, p. 16.

under the circumstances." Said the other, "I am sorry that you are under the circumstances. The Lord would have us living above circumstances, where he can satisfy our hearts and meet our needs."

We have *victory* through faith. He that believes is able to overcome the world (I John 5:4-5). Paul declares that we are able through faith to quench all the fiery darts of the evil one (Ephesians 6:16). Peter tells us to resist the devil through faith (I Peter 5:9).

We have *peace and joy* through faith. "Believing, ye rejoice," says Peter (I Peter 1:8). Actually, there are eight steps of joy which the Christian takes as a result of his faith:

(1) There was joy when we repented of our sins and turned to God for life (Luke 15:7-10).

(2) There was joy when we believed on Christ (I Peter 1:8).

(3) There was joy when the Holy Spirit came into our heart (Romans 5:1-5; Galatians 5:22).

(4) There is joy when we sow the good seed of the kingdom (Psalm 126:5).

(5) There is joy when we go to God in prayer. "Ask and you shall receive that your joy may be full" (John 16:24).

(6) There is joy when we win someone to Christ. "And there was great joy in that city" (Acts 8:8).

(7) There will be joy when we finish our life work (Acts 20:24).

(8) There will be joy when we come to suffering and death (I Peter 4:13).

Faith, then, is the principle on which we live, for the just shall live by faith; and we walk by faith, not by sight (Romans 1:17; II Corinthians 5:7).

3. *Faith and Supplication.* We are told that when we pray we are to *ask* and *believe* (Matthew 21:22). This faith in praying must be such that we believe that we *receive*. ". . . when ye pray, believe that ye receive them, and ye shall have them" (Mark 11:24). These promises, of course, are for the believer who exercises his faith in prayer; and is in contrast to Paul's

reference, "How then shall they call on him in whom they have not believed?" (Romans 10:14).

Dr. Ironside recounts an experience relative to this in his ministry:

> Visiting in a hospital, I spoke to a poor man of emaciated aspect, whom his friends had been anxious that I should see. He was evidently in a very precarious condition, possibly soon to be summoned from time to eternity. I told him I was anxious to know how he stood as to the great matter of his soul's salvation, and asked if he enjoyed peace with God.
>
> "Oh," was the reply, "I'm all right as to that. *I'm praying all the time.*" And a look of intense self-satisfaction settled on his face.
>
> "Well, my dear fellow, I hope you know what Christ had to do to save such sinners as we are and that you know him as your personal Saviour."
>
> "Oh, that's all right. I've known about Jesus for a long time. I've belonged to a church since I was a boy. I haven't any fear for I'm always praying."
>
> "Well, you see, it is not enough to know *about these things,* and people are not saved by praying. Do you trust in the precious blood of Christ?"
>
> A violent attack of coughing interrupted the conversation. When he was easy again, he said, "I can't talk more to you, sir. It excites me too much. But you needn't fear for me, for I won't forget to pray." With this he turned from me, evidently signifying that the conversation was over, so I could do nothing but retire, leaving on the table some simple gospel tracts in the hope that, as he could still read, they might be used of God for blessing to him.
>
> His case is, I fear, like that of many who put prayer, or other Christian practices, in the place of Christ, whereas the truth is, Christ first, then all these other things; or, in other words, life first, then the needs of the new-born babe.[2]

4. *Faith and Service.* Paul, commending the church at Thessalonica, tells them that he remembers constantly their "work of faith, and labor of love, and patience of hope in our Lord Jesus Christ" (I Thessalonians 1:3). Jesus says, "He that believeth on me, the works that I do shall he do also; and greater works than these shall he do; because I go unto my Father" (John 14:12). Faith, then, must be exercised constantly if we are

---

2 H. A. Ironside, *Illustrations of Bible Truth,* pp. 83-84.

to accomplish Christ's work. When the disciples inquired of Jesus why they had failed in casting out a devil, he answered, "Because of your unbelief" (Matthew 17:20). He then told them that if they had faith as a grain of mustard seed, they should be able to remove a mountain. To tear up, to uproot, or to pulverize mountains were all common metaphors for removing difficulties. What Jesus is saying to his followers is simply this: "If you have faith enough, all difficulties can be solved, and even the hardest task can be accomplished."

Faith, however, with all its fruits, is nonexistent for the individual who is unwilling to take God at his word and trust Christ as Saviour. Several years ago the Bush Sanitarium in Louisville caught fire from the center of the building, and the firemen were heroically risking their lives to save the inmates. They were unable to rescue all of them by means of ladders, however; so four firemen secured a net and called for patients standing at the windows to jump. "Now, leap one at a time, and we will save you," they cried.

One after another, three of the men jumped into the net and were saved; but a fourth man cried, "I cannot risk that. Is there some other way?" The firemen frantically pleaded with him to jump, for all the ladders were in use. But he refused, and turned back into the building. Suddenly, from the crowd of onlookers a voice cried out, "Leap out! Leap out of there! They'll save you! Leap out!" The man would not risk the jump, and later, when the fire had been extinguished, firemen found his charred body in the ruins. He had failed to trust his life to the firemen and the net.

Many are like him today. They refuse to plunge by faith into the arms of Jesus, and as a result the flames of eternal punishment await them.

CHAPTER SIX

Regeneration: "Ye Must Be Born Again"

"Jesus . . . said unto him, Verily, verily, I say unto thee, Except a man be born again, he cannot see the kingdom of God" (John 3:3).

MANY YEARS AGO an anti-Christian lecturer had offered an address which he considered a masterpiece. In it he attempted to discount the Bible and had declared the story of Jesus Christ to be a myth. When he had finished speaking, a miner stood up and said, "Sir, I am only a working man, and I don't know what you mean by the word 'myth.' But can you explain me? Three years ago I had a miserable home; I neglected my wife and children; I cursed and swore; I drank up all my wages. Then someone showed me the love of God and of his Son Jesus Christ. And now all is different. We have a happy home; I love my wife and children; I feel better in every way; and I have given up drinking. A new power has taken possession of me since Christ came into my life. Sir"—and his face was all aglow— "can you explain me, aside from Christ?"

D. L. Moody once said, "I was twenty years old before I ever heard a sermon on regeneration. I was always told to be good, but you might as well tell a black man to be white without telling him how. You might tell a slave to be free, but that would not make him free. Christ frees us, however, when we are born again by the power of his Spirit."

We shall study in this chapter: the *call* for regeneration; the *character* of regeneration; the *channels* of regeneration; the *conflict* after regeneration.

I. *THE CALL FOR REGENERATION*

Why is regeneration so necessary? Why did Jesus say to Nicodemus, a good man, "Ye *must* be born again"?

First, regeneration is necessary because the natural man has an incurably wicked nature. The Greek word *anothen*, which is here translated *again*, has several different meanings. It can mean *from the beginning, completely, radically;* it can mean *again,* in the sense of *for the second time;* it can also be translated *from above,* signifying *from God.* Jesus, then, was declaring to Nicodemus that there must be a radical change which can come only from God.

Paul declares that "the carnal mind is at enmity against God; for it is not subject to the law of God, neither indeed can it be. So then they that are in the flesh cannot please God" (Romans 8:7-8). Jeremiah had this same thought in mind when he asked, "Can the Ethiopian change his skin, or the leopard his spots? then may ye also do good, that are accustomed to do evil" (Jeremiah 13:23).

Dr. W. Herschel Ford tells this story:

A young man broke his mother's heart and wrecked his wife's life. He would get a job, but soon lose it through drinking and gambling. His family helped him out many times, but always he would drift back into his old sinful life. One day he said to a Christian friend, "I would like to go to South America and start life over again." The Christian answered, "The first person you would meet down there would be your old self— all the old habits and the old sins would be there with you. No outward condition, no new environment can help you. There is only one way in which you can win the victory and that is through Jesus Christ the Lord. You must be born again." The Christian's message went like an arrow to the poor fellow's heart. He turned away in repentance from his sin and trusted Jesus Christ for salvation and for victory over sin. In a little while he was a new man, made over by the power of God.

The Greek word for *sin* is *hamartia.* It literally means "to miss." A man shoots his gun at the target; he misses—that is *hamartia.* We have missed the marks; we cannot measure up.

Why? because of our wicked natures. We need, therefore, a power to overcome, to change, this sinful nature, and only a supernatural power can do it!

Second, regeneration is necessary because the natural man is spiritually dead. In the parable of the good Samaritan, Jesus tells the story of a man who was left half dead—physically alive, but spiritually dead. The natural man is dead in sins, dead to God. There needs to be the quickening power of God. "And you hath he quickened, who were dead in trespasses and sins" (Ephesians 2:1).

This second chapter of Ephesians is replete with graphic descriptions of the condition of unregenerate man:

We were dead in sin (v. 1).

We lived according to the world (v. 2).

We are servants of the flesh (v. 3).

We were children of wrath (v. 3).

We were without Christ (v. 12).

We were aliens (v. 12).

We were strangers (v. 12).

We were without hope (v. 12).

We were without God (v. 12).

We were afar off (v. 13).

We were at enmity with God (v. 16).

Through regeneration, then, God supplies life when there is none and gives us the hope of glory. It is then that the one who is regenerated may claim the fruits of the Holy Spirit's work, as revealed in this same chapter:

We are quickened (v. 1).

We are saved (v. 5).

We are raised (v. 6).

We are seated (v. 6).

We are created in Christ (v. 10).

We are made nigh unto God (v. 13).

We are made one (v. 14).

We are made new (v. 15).

We are reconciled (v. 16).

We have access to God (v. 18).

We are fellow citizens (v. 19).

We are fitly framed together (v. 21).

We are an habitation of God (v. 22).

Third, regeneration is necessary because the natural man is a child of the devil. "Jesus said unto them, If God were your Father, ye would love me. Ye are of your father the devil, and the lusts of your father ye will do" (John 8:42, 44). Jesus chooses two characteristics of the devil: he is a murderer, and he is a liar; and no murderer or liar has any part in the kingdom of heaven. Since children of the devil inherit their parents' characteristics, then there must of necessity be a change through regeneration.

II. *THE CHARACTER OF REGENERATION*

What is involved in this rebirth which comes only through the power of the Holy Spirit?

First, it is *a new creation*, not a changed nature but a new nature. This is in absolute contrast with the incurably wicked nature of man. We are reminded that "in Christ [we are] a new creation" (II Corinthians 5:17); and that we are "partakers of the divine nature" (II Peter 1:4).

This results in a complete change. Ballintyne Booth, while awaiting trial on a burglary charge, read a sermon by D. L. Moody in a St. Louis paper. The sermon resulted in his conversion; and the authorities noted such a change in the man that when the case came to trial it was dismissed. Booth went to New York but later returned to St. Louis. He was approached by the sheriff who said, "We have shadowed you for six months, and now we are convinced you are an honest man. Therefore, I want you to serve as deputy sheriff."

For more than ten years, until his death, Booth served in this capacity. On one occasion he was asked to speak in a church service; but the sheriff was unable to grant him permission, for he had to appoint a guard for a jewelry store where there was a large stock of diamonds of which no inventory had been taken, and "Booth is the only man I can trust for such a responsibility."

Second, regeneration is a spiritual resurrection, *a new life*. This is in contrast with man's spiritually dead condition before he is born again. We are told that "You hath he quickened who were dead in trespasses and sins" (Ephesians 2:1). Further, John 5:25 declares "the dead . . . that hear shall live." Peter writes that he has "begotten us again . . . by the resurrection of Christ" (I Peter 1:3). This rebirth lifts a man out of this world of space and time, out of this world of sin and defeat, and brings him here and now into living touch with eternity and with eternal life.

Sophocles wrote: "Not to be born at all—that is by far the best fortune; the second best is as soon as one is born with all speed to return thither whence one has come." The poet evidently knew nothing of the experience of a new birth in Christ.

Third, regeneration not only involves a new creation, a spiritual resurrection, but it also *makes one a child of God.* This is in contrast to Jesus' condemnation, "Ye are of your father the devil." Galatians 3:26 states, "ye are all the children of God through faith." John asserts that those who receive Christ are "become the sons of God" (John 1:12).

Fourth, regeneration *admits one into the kingdom of God.* "[He] hath delivered us from the power of darkness, and hath translated us into the kingdom of his dear Son" (Colossians 1:13).

Dr. James Gray relates that at the age of fourteen he was confirmed by the bishop and was taught that he had become "a child of God, a member of Christ, and an inheritor of the kingdom." However, upon his conversion some eight years later, he realized that it was then he became an inheritor of the kingdom. He gives some details of his conversion:

> I was reading a book by William Arnot, *Laws from Heaven for Life on Earth.* My eye fell upon this sentence, "Every soul not already won to Jesus is already lost." It was an arrow of conviction to my soul. An overwhelming sense of my lost and hopeless condition fell upon me, and my soul was hanging over the abyss. I had absolutely no plea but for mercy. Daily I had said my prayers since childhood, but that night, like Saul of Tarsus, I really prayed. The blessed Saviour placed upon my lips: "God be merciful to me a sinner!" In my agony I uttered it with my face upon the floor. And God heard it. That night he lifted me up out of the miry clay and planted me upon a rock.

He put a new song in my mouth, which I have been singing ever since, even salvation unto my God.

III. *THE CHANNELS OF REGENERATION*

Who or what are the agents of regeneration? By what means is one born again?

First, the *Holy Spirit* is the divine person who regenerates. We are informed through the beloved John that we are "born of the Spirit" and "it is the Spirit that quickeneth" (John 3:5, 8; 6:63). The value of anything depends on its aim. Someone has said, "All human things are trivial if they exist for nothing beyond themselves. If we eat food simply for the sake of eating food, we become gluttons, and it is likely to do us far more harm than good; if we eat food to sustain life, to do our work better, and to maintain the fitness of our body at its highest peak, then food has a real meaning and significance." The things of the flesh gain their value only through the Spirit. There is no purpose to life aside from this quickening power. The work of the Holy Spirit is important in this respect; for without it there is no conversion, no new birth, no regeneration, no hope of eternal life.

Second, the *word of God* is the instrument of regeneration. We are "born again . . . by the word of God" (I Peter 1:23); and James tells us that "He begat us by the word of truth" (James 1:18). Water is used as a symbol of the word of God. Paul speaks of Jesus as sanctifying and cleansing those who are his redeemed by "the washing of water by the word" (Ephesians 5:26). Jesus, referring to the members of his body as branches, declares, "Now ye are clean through the word which I have spoken unto you" (John 15:3).

An old professor of biology would hold a little brown seed in his hand. "I know just exactly the composition of the seed. It has nitrogen, hydrogen, and carbon. I know the exact proportions. I can make a seed that will look exactly like it. But if I plant my seed it will come to naught; its elements will simply be absorbed in the soil. If I plant the seed God made, it will become a plant, because it contains the mysterious principle which we call the life principle." The Bible looks like other books, and we cannot altogether understand its marvelous and magnetic power. We do know, however, that when the word of God is planted in good ground, it shows that it has the life principle contained within it; for it brings forth spiritual life; it bears fruit.

E. L. Langston illustrates this point well: "There is a strange plant in Jamaica which is called the 'life plant' for it is almost impossible to kill or destroy any portion of it. When a leaf is cut off and hung by a string, instead of shriveling up and dying like any other leaf, it sends out white threadlike roots and thus gathers moisture from the air and begins to grow new leaves.

The Bible is the life plant of the moral and spiritual world. Circulate . . . it anywhere, and it will soon take root in the . . . heart of mankind and send out tendrils of life."

Dr. R. A. Torrey once said, "No other book has the power to make us acquainted with God and with his Son, Jesus Christ. Study the word that brings eternal life; make it in your own experience the 'implanted word', which is able to save your souls."

Third, our *faith* is necessary for regeneration. We are "children of God by faith in Christ Jesus" (Galatians 3:26). John declares that "whosoever believeth that Jesus is the Christ is born of God" (I John 5:1). A native of India was shown, through a microscope, the germs in the water from a river. He was told not to drink the water any longer. Infuriated, he took a heavy club and smashed the microscope—and continued to drink the water. There is no new birth aside from repentance and faith. Man may spurn this, he may refuse to accept it, he may attempt to dispel the very thoughts of it from his mind; but the fact remains that faith must be exercised before regeneration comes.

IV. THE CONFLICT AFTER REGENERATION

Because the new nature cannot completely replace the old nature, there is often a conflict between the two. Both natures dwell in the believer and continually contend for the mastery. An old Indian once described it by declaring that a white dog and a black dog seemed to be continually fighting each other.

When someone asked which dog won in the fight, he replied, "The one I say 'sic-im' to."

We are exhorted in Galatians to "Walk in the Spirit, and ye shall not fulfill the lust of the flesh. For the flesh lusteth against the Spirit, and the Spirit against the flesh; and these are contrary the one to the other; so that ye cannot do the things that ye would. But if ye be led of the Spirit, ye are not under the law" (Galatians 5:16-18).

Paul further emphasizes this truth in Romans: "For that which I do I allow not; for what I would, that do I not; but what I hate, that do I. If then I do that which I would not, I consent unto the law that it is good. Now it is no more I that do it, but sin that dwelleth in me. For I delight in the law of God after the inward man; but I see another law in my members, warring against the law of my mind, and bringing me into captivity to the law of sin which is in my members" (Romans 7:15-17, 22-23).

We possess the old nature when we are born; the new nature is ours when we are born again. The old nature is of the flesh, the new nature is of the Spirit. "That which is born of the flesh is flesh; and that which is born of the Spirit is spirit" (John 3:6).

The old nature does no good. "There is none that doeth good, no, not one" (Romans 3:12). The new nature does righteousness (I John 2:29).

The old nature cannot please God. "So then they that are in the flesh cannot please God" (Romans 8:8). The new nature cannot commit sin. "We know that whosoever is born of God sinneth not" (I John 5:18).

The old nature loves the world (I John 2:15); the new nature loves God (I John 4:19).

The old nature loves the world (1 John 2:15); the new nature overcomes the world (I John 5:4).

Reaction to this new birth experience is not always the same. In Acts 16 we have the story of two conversions. It took an earthquake to convert the jailer, but the heart of Lydia opened like a flower to the Sun of Righteousness.

Ike Miller was the terror of a North England mining district.

He came to a revival meeting conducted by Henry Moorhouse with the intention of breaking it up. The message of God's love, however, reached his sinful heart, and he was born again by the Spirit of God. Gathering his wife and children around him he asked for their forgiveness for all the harsh words which he had spoken and the ill deeds he had done. Then, as they clasped hands, he prayed,

> Gentle Jesus, meek and mild,
> Look upon a little child;
> Pity my simplicity,
> Suffer me to come to thee.

CHAPTER SEVEN

Redemption: "I Have Been Redeemed"

"Who gave himself for us, that he might redeem us
from all iniquity, and purify unto himself a peculiar
people, zealous of good works" (Titus 2:14).

MAHATMA GANDHI once asked some missionaries who visited him
during one of his fasts to sing a hymn for him. When they inquired concerning his preference, he replied, "Sing the hymn
that expresses all that is deepest in your faith." They sang Sir
Isaac Watts's immortal hymn, "When I Survey the Wondrous
Cross," which truly expresses the entire meaning of the Christian life; for it is Christ's death on the cross which has obtained
eternal redemption for us.

The great doctrine of redemption deserves our closest attention.
Let us examine the following five factors of redemption: the
call for redemption; the *connotation* of redemption; the *compass*
of redemption; the *content* of redemption; the *cost* of redemption.

I. THE CALL FOR REDEMPTION

The Unitarian and others like him say that man is inherently
good, and that by his own efforts he can save himself. The
Bible however, refutes this view, declaring that man is committed
to and a captive of sin, condemned and cursed because of sin,
and compelled to be controlled by sin.

1. *Man is committed to and a captive of sin.* The prophet
says that men have sold themselves for naught (Isaiah 52:3);

and Paul declares that the devil has set a snare and takes men captive at his will (II Timothy 2:26). He also states that men are servants of sin and sold under sin (Romans 6:20; 7:14). Man is thus in complete bondage with no power to escape by himself from sin and the devil.

2. *Man is condemned and cursed because of sin.* Man has broken God's law and a curse is therefore upon him. "For as many as are of the works of the law are under the curse; for it is written, Cursed is everyone that continueth not in all things which are written in the book of the law to do them" (Galatians 3:10). "And the commandment . . . [was] unto death" (Romans 7:10).

The passage here depicts, as it were, a court scene. Man is accused of his crimes, and the death sentence is passed upon him. God, who is completely holy and just, is the policeman who has apprehended him, the district attorney who has charged him, the chief witness who has testified against him, the jury who has tried him, and the judge who has sentenced him. He has received a fair trial, and because of his sins is sentenced to death, "for the wages of sin is death" (Romans 6:23). Under the law he stands condemned; as for righteousness, he has none in God's sight. Man, therefore, needs something outside the law and his own self-righteousness.

3. *Man is compelled to be controlled by sin.* The great apostle continually recounts the struggle of the two natures. He says, "For the good that I would I do not; but the evil which I would not, that I do" (Romans 7:19). The strong power of sin not only controls man, but it seems that the more he struggles with every effort to break sin's power, the more it binds him. By himself he is utterly hopeless; and there must be a power greater than anything he finds within himself to redeem him from the curse which is upon him.

II. *THE CONNOTATION OF REDEMPTION*

The full meaning of redemption offered through Christ would exhaust our finite language if we attempted to describe it. But a better understanding, of all that is involved in this wonderful work of God can be obtained through a study of Old Testament types. Exodus is the book of redemption, and the redemption of Exodus includes the following characteristics:

(1) It is entirely of God.

(2) It is through a person.

(3) It is by blood.

(4) It is by power.

New Testament redemption contains these also. For it is through Christ, by the shedding of his blood, provided through the love of God, and made possible through his mighty power.

Old Testament redemption of the kinsman is also a beautiful picture of New Testament redemption:

(1) The redeemer must be a kinsman.

(2) The redemption is of persons, and offers an inheritance.

(3) The redeemer must be able to redeem.

(4) The kinsman-redeemer must pay the just demand in full.

This, also, pictures Christ and his redemption. He redeems us and offers us an inheritance: "In whom [Christ] we have redemption through his blood . . . also we have obtained an inheritance" (Ephesians 1:7, 11). He became our kinsman through his identification with man (Hebrews 2:14-15). He was able to redeem (John 10:11, 18). He paid the just demand in full: ". . . a lamb without blemish and without spot" (I Peter 1:19); "Christ hath redeemed us from the curse of the law, being made a curse for us" (Galatians 3:13).

There are three New Testament words which are translated "redeem," and a study of their meanings in the original Greek gives us a deeper understanding of redemption:

1. *Agorazo* — to purchase; a slave is bought *in* the market. I Corinthians 6:20 declares, "Ye are bought [redeemed] with a price." Revelation 5:9, referring to Jesus, says, "Thou hast redeemed us to God by thy blood." Here we have the picture of the slave on the auction block, ready to be sold, when a buyer offers the price of redemption and buys the slave in the market.

2. *Ex agorazo* — to buy out; a slave is taken *out of* the market. Galatians 3:13 says, "Christ hath redeemed us from the curse of the law, being made a curse for us; for it is written, Cursed is

everyone that hangeth on a tree." Again, this same book declares, "But when the fullness of the time was come, God sent forth his Son, made of a woman, made under the law, to redeem them that were under the law, that we might receive the adoption of sons" (Galatians 4:4-5). The transaction here progresses a step further. The buyer not only pays the redemption price and purchases the slave in the market; but he also takes the slave away from the market.

3. *Lutroo* — to set free; a slave is loosed and *made free.* This meaning is implied in Titus 2:14, "Who [Jesus] gave himself for us, that he might redeem us from all iniquity, and purify unto himself a peculiar people, zealous of good works." The transaction is now complete; for the buyer has paid the necessary price and has bought the slave in the market; he has taken the slave out of the market; and he has then set him free.

Christ, through the purchase price of his blood, pays the price necessary to redeem us in the market of sin. He takes from us the curse and penalty which was upon us; and we are set free.

III. *THE COMPASS OF REDEMPTION*

A man once stated during the course of his testimony, "When Christ saved me, he saved me all over!" He meant by this that Christ had not only redeemed his soul and spirit but had also given him assurance that the body was to be redeemed. He also emphasized that Christ had saved him from the *penalty* of sin, was now saving him from the *power* of sin, and would some day save him from the *presence* of sin.

1. *There is redemption for the spirit.* The psalmist says, "Into thine hand I commit my spirit; thou hast redeemed me, O Lord God of truth" (Psalm 31:5). A new Spirit is now within us, seeking to fulfill the law of Christ. It is this Spirit which changes the very nature of man.

A man of bad character in his community spent his time gambling, drinking and living a profligate life. His wife and children lived in an alley, suffering continually for want of food and clothing. His wife also suffered much physical abuse as a result of his drunken rage. But one Sunday he was converted; and after this he went to work, saved his money, and moved his family to a nice neighborhood.

Their pastor, visiting them one day, asked the man this question: "Does Christ have the power to make a bad man good?"

Without a word he rose and went to his wife. Taking her hand in one of his, he passed the fingers of his other hand over a scar on her arm. "Do you remember the morning I put that there?" he asked. "Yes," was his wife's reply, "but I have forgiven you, and it is all right."

He then pointed to another scar on her neck. "Do you remember my coming home after drinking and gambling all night and striking you there?" She again replied, "I remember it, but I have long since forgiven you."

He kissed her and then said tenderly, "Dear, I will never do that again. I am a different man now." Then he said to his pastor: "Preacher, you can tell the whole world that Christ has the power to make a bad man good."

2. *There is redemption for the soul.* Psalm 49:8-9 tells us that ". . . the redemption of their soul is precious. . . ."

3. *There will be redemption for the body.* Our bodies belong to God after he has redeemed our souls. "For ye are bought with a price; therefore glorify God in your body, and in your spirit, which are God's (I Corinthians 6:20). We must await that day when Christ shall return before the redemption of our bodies is complete. Paul speaks of this in Romans 8:23, ". . . but ourselves, also, which have the firstfruits of the Spirit, even we ourselves groan within ourselves, waiting for the adoption, to wit, the redemption of our body."

IV. *THE CONTENT OF REDEMPTION*

1. Redemption involves *forgiveness,* for the death of Christ *removes* all hindrances to God's saving of sinners. Ephesians 1:7 declares that it is Christ ". . . in whom we have redemption through his blood, the forgiveness of sins, according to the riches of his grace."

This forgiveness is freely provided for all men, but it must be sought through repentance toward God and faith in Jesus Christ. God does not offer an automatic pardon to all men through the death of his Son; but when any man seeks pardon it is gladly given.

Our daughter one day had misbehaved, and when I counseled with her she began to cry as if she had already been punished. When I told her that she would receive no corporal punishment, she momentarily was happy at the announcement. However, I then informed her that she was to go to her room, and that she must remain there until ready to seek forgiveness.

We left her in her room for the entire evening, and finally, when she could bear it no longer, she came into the room and cried, "Please forgive me. I'm sorry that I have disobeyed. Please forgive me; I won't disobey again."

When she asked for forgiveness, I placed my arms around her and said, "Certainly we will forgive you. Now, we are friends again." With a great sigh she placed her head on my shoulder and said, "I'm glad that's over, for now I feel I'm a member of the family again."

2. Redemption includes *justification,* for the death of Christ *represents* obedience to God's holy law. Paul tells us that we are ". . . justified freely by his grace through the redemption that is in Christ Jesus" (Romans 3:24).

God's laws have been broken by us and these sins must be punished. Christ, who knew no sin, took upon himself the judgment which was on us in order that we may be justified in God's sight. Someone has said that when Christ's atoning blood is applied to our sins, then we are without condemnation, and it is "just as if I'd never sinned."

3. Redemption implies *sanctification,* for the death of Christ *reconciles* us to God and *ratifies* regeneration for us. Reconciliation results when enmity is removed. The believer is set apart at conversion and his trespasses are no longer imputed to him. The penalty of sin, of course, is removed. This is *positional* sanctification. As he progresses in the Christian life after conversion he is able continually to overcome the power of sin which is ever present with us. This is *progressive* sanctification. When Christ returns, the body will be redeemed and we shall be removed from the very presence of sin. This is *perfect* sanctification.

4. Redemption indicates *adoption,* for the death of Christ *redeems* us in order that God may adopt us. ". . . God sent forth his Son . . . to redeem them that were under the law, that we might receive the adoption of sons" (Galatians 4:4-5).

Our daughter came into our family when she was only three months old. She was legally adopted and her birth certificate was changed to include our name. During her first few weeks of public school at the age of six, she was taunted by a classmate who spoke disparagingly of the fact that she had been adopted. The child was deeply hurt as a result, and many tears were shed.

I attempted to explain to her the meaning of adoption, and, although I am sure that she could not yet fully understand all that this implied, she became proud of the fact that she was adopted. She was heard to say one day to a friend, "Your mother and father had to take you when you arrived, but my folks picked me out."

Now that she is older and has accepted Christ as her personal Saviour, I have endeavored to explain to her the full meaning of adoption as it pertains to the children of God.

Many of our states have stringent inheritance laws which protect the rights of an adopted child. Although a child who is one's flesh and blood may be disinherited, an adopted child can never be disinherited in these states. When that child takes his parents' name through legal processes, he becomes forever their heir. It is thus with God. He has ordained that his adopted children shall be joint heirs with his only begotten Son, Jesus.

5. Redemption incorporates *freedom,* for the death of Christ *realizes* for us the great love of God, and we are offered liberty through his Son. "Christ hath redeemed us from the curse of the law" (Galatians 3:13).

Occasionally, a slave was set free in this manner: A man attending an auction would purchase a slave in the name of his own particular god. The transaction paper then stated that the slave was sold to a certain god who had paid the redemption price for him. He now belonged only to this god who had set him free from every other master, and he could never be sold into slavery again. He belonged, body and soul, to the god who bought him.

Paul tells us that we were slaves to five masters: sin, the law, the flesh, the ways of the world, and death. However, Christ through his death on the cross, paid the purchase price of redemption. The moment, then, that we repent of our sin and commit ourselves to Christ, we are redeemed from all former masters, having only one master, Jesus Christ.

V. THE COST OF REDEMPTION

It cost Christ his own blood to redeem us. "But he was wounded for our transgressions, he was bruised for our iniquities; the chastisement of our peace was upon him; and with his stripes we are healed" (Isaiah 53:5).

He suffered at his *birth* in his condescending to take upon himself human flesh (Philippians 2:7). He also suffered at his birth because of the conditions under which he was born (Luke 2:7).

He suffered in his *bout with Satan.* Christ was subject to hunger and thirst and temptation as we are. He withstood Satan and came forth victorious after the temptation in the wilderness (Matthew 4:1-11).

He suffered because of the *bigotry of religious leaders.* They were determined not only to reject him themselves, but also to turn the minds and hearts of others against him (Matthew 26:3-5; Luke 22:63-71; John 11:47-53; 18:12-14).

He suffered because of the *blindness of men.* They heard the immortal words which he spoke; they witnessed the miracles which he performed; yet many, because of the hardness of their hearts, would not believe.

He suffered at his *betrayal.* One of his chosen twelve betrayed him for gain! False accusations were made against him. The very creatures whom God created and made in his own image falsely testified against him (Matthew 26:59-66; Mark 14:53-65).

Jesus suffered at his *brutal trial.* He was mocked and scourged, treated as the worst of criminals. All the gospel writers graphically depict the indignities which were heaped upon the Son of God. Isaiah's prophecy culminates in a description of his suffering through his *broken and bruised body* upon the cruel cross.

A news story recounted the death of an Oklahoma man. Doctors decided that his death was due to malnutrition. Yet when he was examined it was discovered that more than one thousand dollars were in his pockets. Many are dying today, spiritually destitute, when all the resources of God can be theirs through Christ's wonderful redemption!

CHAPTER EIGHT

Sanctification: "Take Time to Be Holy"

"And the very God of peace sanctify you wholly . . ."
(I Thessalonians 5:23)

A LADY APPROACHED a well-known minister after he had delivered a powerful sermon and said to him, "Sir, I appreciate the wonderful message which you have just given; however, I have a question: Are you sanctified?" With a smile, he replied, "Madam, my sanctification is actually in three tenses: I have been sanctified; I am being sanctified; and I shall be sanctified." The lady seemed puzzled. "I do not quite understand you, sir. What I should like to know is, have you had the second blessing?" The minister of Christ answered, "Yes, I have had the second blessing and many more than that."

He was right, for a thorough study of the doctrine of sanctification reveals that it actually is in three tenses. There is evidently much lack of understanding of its fullest meaning; and this is due, no doubt, to a lack of teaching concerning its significance and application.

The basic meaning of sanctification is "to be separate" or "to be set apart." By it a person or thing is separated from one use or purpose and set aside to another use or purpose. The idea as verb or noun is expressed repeatedly in the scriptures. The verb "sanctify" is used 133 times in both the Old and New Testaments. The noun "sanctification" is used six times in the New Testament only. In the Old Testament the term is applied to days, places, utensils, and persons. In the New Testament it is used in reference to Christ and to believers in him. Our study here

77

will have to do with sanctification as it applies to the believer in Christ, as it pertains not only to the beginning of the Christian life, but also to its development and ultimate perfected redemption.

Sanctification of the believer is threefold: positional, progressive, and perfect. Remembering the words of the minister, we see then that the believer is sanctified in the past, the present, and the future.

I. *POSITIONAL SANCTIFICATION*

By positional sanctification we refer to our standing with God, not to our character. God has set aside the believer unto himself; we stand before him as perfected in Christ, who is himself our sanctification. Paul refers to the members of the church at Corinth as "sanctified in Christ Jesus, called to be saints, with all that in every place call upon the name of Jesus Christ our Lord, both theirs and ours. . .[Ye are] in Christ Jesus, who of God is made unto us wisdom, and righteousness, and sanctification, and redemption" (I Corinthians 1:2, 30). Positionally, the weakest believer has the same relationships in grace as the most distinguished saint. As we shall see later, we may grow *in* grace, but not *into* grace.

When does this sanctification take place? It comes about at the moment of our conversion. Paul, in giving his testimony before Agrippa, tells how God called him to preach to the Gentiles "to open their eyes, and to turn them from darkness to light, and from the power of Satan unto God, that they may receive forgiveness of sins, and inheritance among them which are sanctified by faith . . ." (Acts 26:18). This positional sanctification comes between "washing" and "justification" as expressed in I Corinthians 6:11: "Such were some of you; but ye are washed, but ye are sanctified, but ye are justified in the name of the Lord Jesus, and by the Spirit of our God."

Referring to the sequence of this text, which he used as the basis for a sermon, Dr. Ironside recounts the following:

> At the close (of the message) a dignified personage came to me and said, "Do you know, you got your theology terribly mixed tonight?"

"Did I?" I said. "Straighten me out."

"You put sanctification before justification. You have to be justified and then you get the second blessing."

"Pardon me, but you are mistaken," I said. "I did not put sanctification before justification."

"You most certainly did."

"I most certainly did not; it was the Apostle Paul who did."

"Why, you cannot blame your wrong theology on him."

"I was simply quoting scripture."

"You misquoted it. It reads, 'Ye are justified, ye are sanctified.' "

"No, no," I said. "Read it."

And he began to read, "But ye are washed, but ye are sanctified, but ye are justified," and then he said, "Why, there is a misprint here. Wait a minute. I will get a Revised Bible."

He got it and looked at it, and read, "Washed, sanctified, justified."

"Why," he said, "I never saw that before; but all I have to say is the Apostle Paul was not clear on the holiness question when he wrote that!"[1]

It is quite evident that the confusion comes about in the misinterpretation of terms and tenses of the scriptures as they pertain to the full meaning of sanctification. So we see then that we are positioned in Christ at conversion. This settles the question of time.

Now, what is the means of this sanctification? It comes through the sacrifice of Christ. ". . . we are sanctified through the offering of the body of Jesus Christ once for all" (Hebrews 10:10). "Wherefore Jesus also, that he might sanctify the people with his own blood, suffered without the gate" (Hebrews 13:12).

Christ is made by God our sanctification. Since holiness is the very nature of God, he makes the believer holy by imputing unto him the holiness of Christ. In him, whom the Father sanctified and sent into the world, God's holiness was revealed incarnate; and thus his holiness was brought within reach of man. Therefore, the only way to become holy is to partake of the holiness of Christ, offered to us through his atoning work on the cross.

---

[1] H. A. Ironside, *I Corinthians*, pp. 86-87.

II. *PROGRESSIVE SANCTIFICATION*

By progressive sanctification we describe the actual daily experience of separation from sin to God.

When does this take place in the life of the Christian? It should take place now and throughout our lives. As one advances higher in spiritual growth in Christ, he learns how to gain strength for withstanding temptation and in living a holy life. "For this is the will of God, even your sanctification. . . . For God hath not called us unto uncleanness, but unto holiness" (I Thessalonians 4:3, 7).

It becomes necessary for the Christian to grow in grace, to progress in the Christian life, if he is to be used by the Lord. "If a man therefore purge himself from these, he shall be a vessel unto honor, sanctified, and meet for the master's use, and prepared unto every good work" (II Timothy 2:21). "Having therefore these promises, dearly beloved, let us cleanse ourselves . . . perfecting holiness (sanctification) in the fear of God" (II Corinthians 7:1). Paul exhorts us who were once servants of unrighteousness to yield ourselves as the servants of God unto the fruit of holiness (Romans 6:19-22).

We often find ourselves able to pass judgment on how the other fellow should conduct himself; then we fail to measure up within ourselves. A little boy six years of age lived next door to another boy the same age. One day their play developed into a misunderstanding. The quarrel between the boys waxed warm and long. Suddenly, little Edward drew himself up and said, "It's time one of us acted like a Christian. How about you?"

One must continually progress in the Christian life, if he is to please God and influence others. A woman following her conversion, suffered great persecution from her husband. One day she was asked, "When your husband is angry and persecutes you, what do you do?" She replied: "Well, sir, I cook his food better; when he complains, I sweep the floor cleaner; and when he speaks unkindly, I answer him mildly. I try to show him that when I became a Christian, I became a better wife and a better mother." Consequently, the husband, who had withstood the preaching and pleas of the pastor, was unable to withstand the practical preaching of his wife and soon gave his heart to God.

What is the means by which we may progress in the Christian graces? It is through a study of the word of God. It becomes necessary for the Christian to dwell constantly upon the word and obey its teachings. Jesus, in his great high priestly prayer, called upon the Father to "Sanctify them through thy truth; thy word is truth" (John 17:17). Paul, speaking of the church, declared that Christ gave himself for it in order that "he might sanctify and cleanse it with the washing of water by the word" (Ephesians 5:26).

A well-known contemporary evangelist has prepared a sermon titled "Worshipping St. Vitus." Truly, this title captures the spirit of the times in which we live. Many professing Christians are so busy with so many things; consequently, they take no time to commune with God through meditation upon his word and intercessory prayer. As a result, there is little power to withstand temptation, and much service which is rendered comes only from the energy of the flesh. More than anything else, we need to come apart and commune with God. This is our only hope if we are to receive spiritual sustenance to do the will of God. Someone has aptly declared, "Come apart and rest awhile, or you will come apart." An old divine once said, "I should as soon expect a farmer to prosper in business who contented himself with sowing his fields and never looking at them till harvest, as expect a believer to attain much holiness who was not diligent about his Bible reading, his prayers, and the use of his Sundays. Our God . . . works by means, and he will never bless the soul of that man who pretends to be so high and spiritual that he can get on without them."

We are told by scientists that the most violent storms on the ocean disturb the water to only a few hundred feet below the surface. The hurricane, which can cause the raging waves resulting in shipwreck and disaster, is unable to affect the depths. Below the turbulent waves there is peace. In a similar way, one may find peace and victory through the depths of God's word in the midst of all disrupting circumstances of life.

Andrew Murray has said of meditation, "Little of the word with little prayer is death to the spiritual life. Much of the word with little prayer gives a sickly life. Much prayer with little of the word gives emotional life. But a full measure of both the word and prayer each day gives a healthy and powerful life."

As a result of these daily practices, the Holy Spirit is able to work through the believer to a greater extent, and the fruit of the Spirit is manifested. Notice these nine graces as they are given in Galatians 5:22-23: love, joy, peace, longsuffering, gentleness, goodness, faith, meekness, and temperance. There are three considerations here:

(1) *Character as an inward state*—love, joy, peace;

(2) *Character in expression toward man* — longsuffering, gentleness, goodness;

(3) *Character in expression toward God*—faith, meekness, temperance.

Taken together these graces present a moral portrait of Christ and may be understood as one definition of fruit as mentioned in John 15:1-8. Such character in the believer is possible only through a vital union to Christ; it is a result of complete submission to the guidance of the Holy Spirit.

III. *PERFECT SANCTIFICATION*

By perfect sanctification we refer to the final and complete work of Christ at his coming when he will remove us from all contact with sin. It is then that our *experience* will correspond with our *position*. This, of course, has not yet come to pass, and will happen only when Christ visibly returns. The Apostle Paul, in speaking of his desire to follow Christ in the power of his resurrection, says, "Not as though I had already attained, either were already perfect; but I follow after, if that I may apprehend that which also I am apprehended of Christ Jesus" (Philippians 3:12). He is looking forward to that time when his redemption will be complete and his sanctification will be perfect. John confirms that this perfect state comes about at the appearing of Christ: "Beloved, now are we the sons of God, and it doth not yet appear what we shall be; but we know that, when he shall appear, we shall be like him; for we shall see him as he is" (I John 3:2).

Paul, again, in expressing his desire that all Christians should abound in love one toward another, implies that this love will be made perfect, "unblameable in holiness toward God, even our Father at the coming of our Lord Jesus Christ" (I Thessalonians 3:13). The word "holiness" is used interchangeably with "sanctification." In the conclusion of this letter to the church at Thessalonica, Paul prays, "And the very God of peace sanctify you wholly; and I pray God your whole spirit and soul and body be preserved blameless unto the coming of our Lord Jesus Christ" (I Thessalonians 5:23). Man is body, soul, and spirit. The human soul and spirit are not identical. The spirit is that part of man which *knows*; therefore, his mind. The soul is the seat of the *affections* and *desires;* therefore, of the *emotions* and active *will*. Although, at our conversion, we are set apart and sealed *unto* the day of redemption, that redemption is completed only when Christ returns. Then the body, as well as the soul and spirit, will be redeemed; our sanctification will be perfect.

This will come about through the mighty power of God. Jude says *he is able* to present us faultless (Jude 24). Paul declares that we look for the Saviour to appear, for when he appears, he will change our vile bodies and will fashion them like unto his glorious body. *He is able.* He alone has the power to do this (Philippians 3:21).

Realizing, then, that it is God who works in us to will and to do of his good pleasure, we should strive always to please him, while we await his return. We should never become overconfident, nor give place to the devil. History records that the English took Quebec from the French because the latter became overconfident. Wolfe, with his English forces, scaled the rocky cliffs and conquered the city because of the carelessness of the French who failed to keep watch. We may progress from day to day in our sanctification only as our hearts and minds are stayed on Christ, remembering that he may return at any time. Jesus himself said, "Watch ye therefore . . . I say unto you all, Watch" (Mark 13:35, 37).

The *Messiah* was first performed in London on March 23, 1743. Among those present in the great audience was the king himself. The throng was deeply moved by the "Hallelujah Chorus", and at the singing of the powerful words, "For the

Lord God omnipotent reigneth," the entire audience, including the king, sprang to its feet, and remained standing through the entire chorus. From that time it has been the custom to stand during the chorus whenever it is performed. It is thus that with great joy our souls stand to salute him "who cometh in the name of the Lord." He is "King of kings, and Lord of lords." To him let us pledge our allegiance!

CHAPTER NINE

The Church: *"A Thousand Years the Same"*

"Christ also loved the church, and gave himself for it . . . that he might present it to himself a glorious church" (Ephesians 5:25, 27).

CAN WE DEFINE the church? "My gypsy tent, if Jesus is in it, is as grand as St. Paul's Cathedral, and St. Paul's Cathedral is nothing but a glorified quarry without Jesus," Gypsy Smith once declared. Christ in the heart of believers in a local fellowship makes the church.

Several analogies are given in the Bible which describe the church and its function:

(1) The church is called a *Building*. "For we are laborers together with God; ye are God's husbandry, ye are God's building" (I Corinthians 3:9). Christ, of course, is the builder of the church: "I will build my church; and the gates of hell shall not prevail against it" (Matthew 16:18). We are told in Ephesians 2:20 that Christ is the chief cornerstone.

(2) The church is referred to as a *Body*. "Now ye are the body of Christ, and members in particular" (I Corinthians 12:27). Christ is the head of the body (Colossians 2:19).

(3) The church is considered to be Christ's *Bride*. ". . . prepared as a bride adorned for her husband" (Revelation 21: 2). Christ is the Bridegroom. John the Baptist said, "He that hath the bride is the bridegroom" (John 3:29).

(4) The church is pictured as *Branches of the Vine*. (John 15:2).

(5) The church is likened to a *Flock* (Luke 12:32), with

Christ as the Shepherd. "I am the good shepherd; the good shepherd giveth his life for the sheep" (John 10:11).

(6) The church is compared to a *Casket of Jewels.* "And they shall be mine, saith the Lord of hosts, in that day when I make up my jewels" (Malachi 3:17).

(7) The church is designated as a *Temple.* "Know ye no that ye are the temple of God, and that the Spirit of God dwelleth in you?" (I Corinthians 3:16). Christ is the High Priest (Hebrews 4:15).

From these illustrations, then, we learn that the church is great in the sight of our Saviour. When the members of the church at Corinth were guilty of things which grieved the Lord, Paul asked the pointed question: ". . . despise ye the church of God?" (I Corinthians 11:22).

Conditions which were prevalent in the Corinthian church are with us today. A leading Christian magazine, after taking a poll among several outstanding religious leaders, came to the conclusion that the present-day church is beset by a multitude of sins, chief of which are: unclean living, undeveloped vision, unconcern for the lost, unrepenting proud spirits, uncultivated devotional lives, unforgiving spirits toward the brethren, and unwillingness to submit to discipline.

Every serious Christian, realizing that Christ loved the church and gave himself for it, will also love Christ and will make his church glorious through consecration, concerted prayer life, concentrated missionary zeal, conscientiousness in stewardship, and concern for souls.

I. *A GLORIOUS CHURCH IS MADE UP OF A CONSECRATED MEMBERSHIP*

There are some professing Christians who have strange ideas concerning discipleship. To be consecrated the child of God must be clean; he must censure all sin and champion right and righteousness; he must cast himself upon the Lord; he should cease from worry; he should cheer the downcast and care for the outcast; he must cherish the word of God and claim the promises of God; he should clothe himself in humility, com-

mitting himself daily to his Father's will and commending his
wonderful salvation to others. As he strives for these attain-
ments, he will surely walk well-pleasing in the Lord.

Too many of us, however, regard the church only as a crutch,
to be used as a support at our convenience. One writer observed
that some people go to church only three times in their entire
lives: when they are hatched, matched, and dispatched.

> Each time I pass a church,
> I stop to make a visit;
> So that when I'm carried in,
> Our Lord won't say, "Who is it?"

Others, while not living fully and significantly dedicated lives,
may attend the services of the church fairly regularly, but because of their spiritual deficiency miss the power of God for
their lives.

> Some go to church to take a walk;
> Some go to church to laugh and talk;
> Some go there to meet a friend;
> Some go there their time to spend.
> Some go there to doze and nod;
> The wise go there to worship God.

The step from the surrender of a sinner to Christ to the act
of real dedication by which a Christian places himself where
God can consecrate him for whatever service he may have for
him is illustrated by the action of Italy during World War II.
Beaten down by the Allies, she surrendered unconditionally.
Later, her leaders declared war on Germany, her former ally.
First, Italy yielded in total surrender, then she allied herself *with*
her former enemies and *against* her former friends.

We recall an incident in which a lady asked her pastor for a
definition of real consecration. "It is signing your name to a
blank sheet of paper," he replied, "and letting the Lord fill in the
details."

Someone has said, "The service of Christ is the business of my
life; the will of Christ is the law of my life; the presence of
Christ is the joy of my life; and the glory of Christ is the crown
of my life." This, then, becomes true consecration.

II. *A GLORIOUS CHURCH WILL CONTINUALLY MAINTAIN A CONCERTED PRAYER EFFORT*

God's word is manifested to the world through the power of prayer. "And when they had prayed, the place was shaken where they were assembled together; and they were all filled with the Holy Ghost, and they spake the word of God with boldness" (Acts 4:31). When a church is a *praying* church, it will also be a *praising* church, ". . . singing and making melody in your heart to the Lord" (Ephesians 5:19); it will be a *producing* church (I John 3:17); and it will be a *preaching* church (Acts 8:4).

O, how we need to pray! The world needs our prayers! And we must believe God when we pray! It has been suggested that prayer is the highest use to which speech can be put. Therefore let us examine some important aspects of prayer as presented in James 4 and 5. Here James gives God's conditions for answered prayer:

(1) *Consecration*, for the friendship of the world is enmity with God (4:4-5). Dr. Simon Blocker declares at this point:

> Prayer is man going through bankruptcy before God and becoming solvent through Divine assets. Prayer is confession of human inability and recourse to God's omnipotence. Prayer is desertion of humanism and a sustained cry for God's inter-position. Prayer is self-crucifixion and crowning Jesus as Lord of all. . . .Prayer is the use of a divinely established technique to effect results in the spiritual redemption of mankind. God tests His church at the point of prayer.[1]

(2) *Contrition*, for God resists the proud and gives grace to the humble (4:6). This indicates that we must have implicit faith in his promises. Vincent says, "Prayer is to be without the element of skeptical criticism, whether of God's character and dealings, or the character and behaviour of those for whom prayer is offered."

(3) *Charity*, for we are not to speak evil one of another (4:11-12).

(4) *Conduct*, for God must order our lives if we are to have power from him (4:13-5:6). Phillips Brooks has said, "Do

---

[1] Simon Blocker, *How to Achieve Personality Through Prayer*, pp. 119-120.

not pray for easy lives! Pray to be stronger men. Do not pray for tasks equal to your powers. Pray for powers equal to your tasks. Then the doing of your work shall be no miracle, but you shall be a miracle."

One writer has expressed it this way:

> Prayer is not a substitute for work; it is a desperate effort to work further and to be efficient beyond the range of one's powers. It is not the lazy who are most inclined to prayer; those pray most who care most, and who, having worked hard, find it intolerable to be defeated.

Prayer should not be seen as an easy way of obtaining what one wants, but as the only way of becoming what God wants us to be.

We should also be practical in our praying. During one of his journeys across the Atlantic, D. L. Moody was told that there was a fire in the hold of the ship. Members of the crew and some passenger volunteers formed a bucket brigade to extinguish the blaze. A friend said, "Mr. Moody, let us go aside and engage in prayer." But the great evangelist replied, "Not so, sir; we stand right here and pass buckets and pray hard all the time."

(5) *Constancy*, for patience has its great reward (5:11). Spurgeon has said, "Delayed answers to prayer are not only trials of faith, but they give us opportunities of honoring God by our steadfast confidence in him under apparent repulses."

(6) *Cooperation*, for we have the blessed privilege of praying for one another in all our needs (5:13-16a). A twelve-year-old girl who had won first place in a national spelling contest was asked if she had prayed that God would help her win. Her reply is a classic expression of God's teaching concerning prayer: "I prayed, but I prayed that the best speller would win."

(7) *Concern*, for God has promised to use our prayerful interest to help save souls (5:16b-20).

Great men before us have given worthy examples of the manifestation of power through prayer. A ship's captain recounts his experience with George Mueller of Bristol. Mueller came to him on a very foggy day, and said, "Captain, I have come to tell you I must be in Quebec Saturday afternoon." When the captain informed him of the impossibility of the undertaking in such weather, the man of prayer replied, "Very well, if your ship cannot take me, God will find some other way. I have never broken an engagement in fifty-seven years. Let us go down into the chart room and pray."

The captain was amazed and protested, "Do you know how dense this fog is?" Mr. Mueller replied, "My eye is not on the density of the fog, but on the living God, who controls every circumstance of life." He knelt down and prayed, and when he had finished he said, "Get up and open the door, and you will find the fog gone." The captain found it so, and on Saturday afternoon George Mueller was in Quebec for his engagement.

God gives as many reasons in his word why prayer may not be answered. We only mention them here, encouraging the reader to give them a thorough examination:

Inattention to mercy (Proverbs 21:13).

Indifference (Proverbs 1:28).

Insubordination (1 Samuel 28:6).

Iniquity (Isaiah 59:2).

Instability (James 1:6-7).

Illicit indulgence (James 4:3).

Idolatry (Ezekiel 14:3).

III. *A GLORIOUS CHRURCH WILL CONTINUALLY CONCENTRATE ON MISSIONARY ZEAL*

No church has a right to exist which does not recognize constantly the all-importance of Christ's Great Commission. Man's need is the same in all the world, for death has passed upon all men in that all have sinned (Romans 3:9, 19; 5:12).

God loves the whole world, and salvation is now offered to the whole world (John 3:16; Romans 10:13). It is his desire that the whole world be saved (I Timothy 2:3-4; 2 Peter 3:9). But God must judge the whole world so the gospel must be preached and accepted (Acts 17:13; Psalm 9:17).

We have the direct command of Jesus to take the gospel to all the world (Matthew 28:19; Acts 1:8; John 20:21). The Communists are willing to give their lives, if necessary, in order to spread their false teachings throughout the world. Shall Christians be content to do less? We have the example of the early church. They counted not their lives as dear. They went every-where preaching the wonderful gospel of grace (Acts 8:4).

It is said that in World War II the British minister of war was able in less than twenty minutes to flash to the entire world the message that Britain had declared war. We have been preaching the message of peace for almost two thousand years. May God help us to keep ever at it, for every witness counts greatly for Christ's glory!

An aerial gunner recounts how Christian natives on a South Pacific island had won to Christ seven navy airmen who had been shot down in combat with the Japanese. The natives had received the gospel from American missionaries before the war. The gunner and two companions reached the island after being at sea on a raft for two and a half days. Four others were al-ready there. For the next eighty-seven days they hid on the Japanese-occupied island, watched over by the natives, whose first act was to give them a Bible. The airmen said, "Every night the natives would gather round us, and we took turns reading the Bible. They sang songs which we knew. You can tell the world that we are now devout Christians." Others may criticize missionary endeavor, but these airmen are praising God that America sent missionaries to the islands of the South Pacific. Christ set the example for us by personally witnessing to all types of people, not only in his home but in other places as well. One president of the United States emphasized the importance of foreign missions when he declared:

> Since becoming President, I have come to know that the finest type of Americans we have abroad today are the missionaries of the cross. I am humiliated that I am not finding out until this late day the worth of foreign missions and the nobility of the missionaries. Their testimony in China, for instance, during the war there, is beyond praise. Their courage is thrilling and their fortitude heroic.

Missions to the ends of the earth are our only hope of spread-ing the gospel of Christ. Let us recognize this and follow Christ's will for our lives, so carrying out the Great Commission.

Robert Moffatt, father-in-law of David Livingstone, when asked to write in an album, penned the following lines:

My album is in savage breasts
Where passions reign and darkness rests
　Without one ray of light.

To write the name of Jesus there,
To point to worlds both bright and fair,
And see the pagan bow in prayer,
　Is all my soul's delight.

IV.　*A GLORIOUS CHURCH IS ONE WHICH IS CONSCIENTIOUS IN STEWARDSHIP*

Stewardship involves the total life: time, talents, and money. We should not only give of our time in service to Christ and his church, but we desperately need to spend time alone with him. God looks to us to be good stewards of our time.

A doctor had advised a patient that her health was bad. "My nerves are bad, too, for I am almost at the breaking point," she later told a friend. Sometime afterward the friend called on her and found that the strained look had left her face, and in its place there was a look of quiet peace. She said she felt better than she had for years. Upon further inquiry, she explained, "When I first became a Christian I tithed my income; now I tithe my time, also. I see to it that he has a tenth of my day for quiet waiting on him. Truly he has undertaken for my every need, and I praise him."

We are also to be good stewards of the talents which we possess. Jesus emphasized the importance of this stewardship in his teachings. It it not how much we have which is so important, but rather what we do with that which is ours.

Reading from George William Curtis one day, a girl came across a statement that read, "An engine of one-cat power, running all the time, is more effective than a forty-horsepower one that is idle." From that time on her life was different. Though she did not have many talents, and no outstanding ones, she kept the little she did have in constant use. Though her life was lived in narrow confines, with little opportunity for outstanding service, she used her one-cat power to its fullest. In later years she became a very busy, useful and influential woman because she was constantly watching for little places in which to serve, narrow places where she was needed.

We are commanded by the Lord to be conscientious in bringing our tithes into the storehouse (Malachi 3:10). He tells us that the tithe is holy, and when we obey him in this respect, we are then in position to receive a full measure of his blessings.

A missionary tells of a church in the orient whose members were all tithers. Because of this they have more for Christian work than any other church in their country. They pay their own pastor, and have sent two missionary families to spread the gospel in a community cut off from the outside world. They are entirely responsible for this work and are very earnest about it. They are intensely interested in all forms of Christian work, especially work for unfortunates of every kind, and their gifts for this kind of work are large. They not only have accepted Christ but, having found him good, are making him known to others. And every member is a leper.

V. *A GLORIOUS CHURCH WILL HAVE A CONCERN FOR SOULS*

The unsaved are everywhere, and the personal witness through Christian love is necessary if they are to be won for Christ. When Christians are willing to meet the conditions which God gives us, then we shall win them one by one. It takes a great deal of faith, faithfulness, enthusiasm, and perseverance to reach the lost for Christ; but it can be done.

Dr. Jerome Williams recalls an incident from his ministry. A small boy had come forward at the invitation at the close of a Sunday service, professing his faith in Christ as his personal Saviour. Some of the older members of the church, however, expressed doubt about the boy's conversion.

That evening, just before service time, Dr. Williams heard a knock on his study door, and when he opened it he found William, the boy who had made profession that morning, standing there. "Come in, William. You look troubled. Do you think you made a mistake this morning in joining the church?"

"No, sir," was his quick reply. "I never did anything in my life that made me happier. I have Fred, my pal, down here, and he is not a Christian. I have been trying all afternoon to lead him to Christ, but I can't quite make it. I want you to help me get him over."

The pastor was soon able to help William "get Fred over"; and at the close of the evening service that day he too confessed Christ publicly. William, overjoyed, came also to stand with Fred, and when the pastor gave him opportunity to say a word, he told how he had worked all the afternoon in his endeavor to lead Fred to Christ. "Pastor helped me get him over," was his simple explanation.

Dr. Williams declared that some adults who apparently had never led a soul to Christ wept openly as they heard the simple testimony of a boy who won another boy less than eight hours after his own conversion.[2]

Summing up, a glorious church is one with an ideal pastor, an ideal people, and an ideal program:

The Ideal Pastor:

    (1) One who preaches the word of God;

    (2) One who proves the worth of God;

    (3) One who practices the will of God.

The Ideal People:

    (1) Those who walk with God;

    (2) Those who work for God;

    (3) Those who worship only God.

The Ideal Program:

    (1) One that is world-wide;

    (2) One that wins to God;

    (3) One that welcomes all.

---

[2] Jerome Williams, *Let Me Illustrate,* pp. 26-29.

CHAPTER TEN

Holy Spirit: *"Breathe on Me"*

> "But the Comforter, which is the Holy Ghost, whom
> the Father will send in my name, he shall teach you
> all things, and bring all things to your remembrance,
> whatsoever I have said unto you" (John 14:26).

SEVERAL LEARNED MEN attempted to persuade a scholar to become
a Christian, but failed. Later in conversing with him, a plain
man who could not boast of high learning referred not to logical
reasoning but to the work of the Holy Spirit. The scholar was
saved and later exclaimed, "When I heard no more than human
reason, I opposed it with human reason; but when I heard the
Spirit I was obliged to surrender." The blessed Holy Spirit is
in the world today, and it is through him that we are given light
on the gospel as it is revealed through God's Word.

A thorough study of the Holy Spirit in one sermon would be
a monumental undertaking, indeed; however, we shall attempt
to cover the subject as well as possible by dividing this message
into three sections: His Personality; His Past and Present; and
His Performances.

I. *HIS PERSONALITY*

1. *He is presented as a person.* Jesus in John 14:26 and
15:26, refers to the Holy Spirit as one who has the power to comfort, to teach, to remind, and to testify. In John 16:7-8 our
Lord, referring to his imminent departure, promises to send the

Spirit who "will reprove the world of sin, and of righteousness, and of judgment." In verses 13 and 14 he alludes to the Spirit as truth, one who guides, one who speaks and hears, and one who has the power to reveal the future.

2. *He possesses the faculties of a person.* We are told that he has intellect. I Corinthians 2:10-11 declares that he has knowledge which he imparts to man. He also possesses emotions, for in Romans 15:30 we are told that he loves; in Ephesians 4:30 we learn that he may be grieved. And we are told that he has a will: "But all these worketh that one and the selfsame Spirit, dividing to every man severally as he will" (I Corinthians 12:11).

3. *He performs what only a person can do.* As we study the scriptures concerning the Holy Spirit, we learn that he speaks, he strives, he supports Christ's divinity, he searches, he strengthens the mind and heart, he selects, he supplies leadership, he solicits in our behalf, he sends forth his servants, and he sanctifies. In the light of all this, R. A. Torrey's words bear great significance: "Anyone who does not know the Holy Spirit as a person has not attained unto a complete and well-rounded experience."

4. *He possesses the attributes of a divine person.* As a member of the Trinity he has the characteristics of the Godhead: He brews 9:14 tells us that he is eternal; in Luke 1:35 the manifestation of his power is apparent; Psalm 139:7-10 declares that he is omnipresent; and in I Corinthians 2:10-11 we learn that he is omniscient. In this last passage he is said to possess "the deep things of God." Jesus refers to him as the "Spirit of truth" and declares that he will guide all believers into all truth (John 16: 12-13).

5. *He may be profaned as only a person can be.* He may be resisted (Acts 7:51); he may be grieved (Ephesians 4:30); he may be quenched (I Thessalonians 5:19); he can be lied to (Acts 5:3); he can be despised (Hebrews 10:29); and he can be blasphemed (Matthew 12:31-32). Resisting him is usually thought to refer to the actions of those whom he endeavors to convict of sin and convince of a need for salvation. The immediate reference to grieving him refers essentially to corrupt speech; however, it may also connote disobedience or spurning

his revealed will. He may be quenched when a child of God attempts service without dependence upon him, or refuses to speak the truth in response to his bidding. That he may be lied to is evidenced by Ananias' conspiracy with his wife to hold back a part of the offering. Peter declared that he had not lied to men, but to the Holy Ghost (Acts 5:3). Hebrews 10:29 refers to men who spurn the Spirit's revelation as those who despise him, and Jesus says in Matthew that those who attribute the work of the Spirit to Satan are guilty of blaspheming him (12:31-32).

II. *HIS PAST AND PRESENT*

Let us look at the persons visited by the Holy Spirit, the purpose of his visits, and the promise left with those he visited as they appear in Old Testament times, during the early life of Jesus, and in present days.

1. *In Old Testament Times*

(1) *The Persons*: He came upon men and left them as he pleased. Judges 6:34 reveals that "the Spirit of the Lord came upon Gideon." Judges 13:25, referring to Samson, declares that "the Spirit of the Lord began to move him at times. . . ." Judges 14:6, 19 also tells of the Spirit coming upon him for special duties; later in the same book we learn that the Spirit came upon him again to give him added strength (15:14); and after he had departed from the Lord, when Delilah cried to him that the Philistines were upon him, he expected the Spirit's power to be upon him, for "he knew not that the Lord was departed from him" (16:20). I Samuel 10:6 and 11:6 relate the Spirit as coming upon Saul; and 16:14 declares that the Spirit departed from him. In Psalm 51:11 David pleads that the Spirit not be taken from him.

(2) *The Purposes*: He accomplished the will of God through men.

He imparted physical strength (Judges 14:5-6; 15:14-15).

He invested men with skill (Exodus 31:1-5).

Connor says in this respect:

> The Old Testament thus represents the Spirit as operative in nature and bestowing extraordinary powers on man in what we ordinarily think of as his natural life. This is in line with Old

Testament monotheism which conceived of the world order and man's powers as all being the creation of God and as being sustained by him.[1]

He instructed and taught men (Nehemiah 9:20; Acts 28:25-27).

He inspired the prophets and the writing of the word (II Peter 1:21; II Samuel 23:2).

(3) *The Promise*: The Old Testament reveals that the Holy Spirit later would be offered to everyone (Zechariah 12:10; Isaiah 44:2-3; Joel 2:28).

2. *During the Earthly Life of Jesus*

(1) *The Persons:* The Holy Spirit is offered to all. "If ye then, being evil, know how to give good gifts unto your children; how much more shall your heavenly Father give the Holy Spirit to them that ask him?" (Luke 11:13). It is evident that up until this time none of Christ's many disciples, with the possible exception of Mary of Bethany, had asked for the Spirit in the faith of this promise.

(2) *The Purposes*: His activities are now more clearly known. Jesus tells Nicodemus that there must be a spiritual birth which can come only through the power of the Holy Spirit (John 3:3, 5-6). Man is to recognize through the Spirit's conviction that he has fallen short of God's holy demands, and that through repentance and faith he may be born again by the power of the Spirit.

(3) *The Promise*: He will come and indwell all believers. "And I will pray the Father, and he shall give you another Comforter, that he may abide with you forever; even the Spirit of truth; whom the world cannot receive, because it seeth him not, neither knoweth him; but ye know him; for he dwelleth with you, and shall be in you" (John 14:16-17). This indwelling of the Spirit comes about at the moment of the new birth. When one is regenerated through the Spirit he then is indwelt by the Spirit.

3. *During This Age*

(1) *The Persons*: He indwells every believer. "For by one Spirit are we all baptized into one body" (I Corinthians 12:13).

[1] W. T. Connor, *The Work of the Holy Spirit*, pp. 22-23.

"What? know ye not that your body is the temple of the Holy Ghost which is in you, which ye have of God, and ye are not your own?" (I Corinthians 6:19).

(2) *The Purposes*: He is building and controlling the church. We are baptized by the Spirit into one body (I Corinthians 12:13); and we are to receive the power of the Holy Spirit for witnessing (Acts 1:8).

(3) *The Promise*: He will abide with us forever (John 14:16).

III. *HIS PERFORMANCES*

His work in the individual may be divided into three stages: before conversion, at conversion, and after conversion.

1. *Before conversion.* He reproves the world of sin, of righteousness, and of judgment (John 16:7-11). It is only through the Spirit's conviction that man may come to the light of the gospel of grace.

Dr. Ralph A. Herring, referring to the light of the Holy Spirit bringing conviction, says:

> Unless one is looking directly towards the light, he does not see it at all except by reflection. On a clear dark night one may stand by a powerful searchlight and, because he cannot see the source of the light, hardly be aware of it at all. Only as dust particles in the atmosphere, moths, or other creatures of the night reflect its rays to him will he recognize the shaft of light which would otherwise lose itself in the illimitable sky above.
>
> This truth was dramatically brought home to me many years ago when I was driving a Model T Ford automobile one night down the steep slopes of the Saluda mountains in South Carolina. It was in the days before roads were well graded and curves along the mountainside carefully indicated by railings painted white. On a particularly steep incline, coming suddenly to a sharp turn, I found myself almost in complete darkness. Thinking that my lights had blown I slammed on my brakes and stopped to consider the emergency. I soon found, however, that my lights were burning as brightly as ever, but facing off from the mountainside. There was nothing to reflect their light so that it could be seen by me.[2]

2 Ralph A. Herring, *God Being My Helper,* pp. 93-94.

He also strives with men, but his pleading may not always continue (Genesis 6:3). Jesus, in offering the Spirit to his disciples, says that the unconverted cannot receive him, for they first must be convicted by him (John 14:17).

2. *At conversion*, he regenerates, indwells, baptizes, and seals. Jesus declares that the new birth comes about by the power of the Spirit (John 3:5). This becomes his work of regeneration.

Paul tells us that we have received the Spirit of God "that we might know the things that are freely given to us of God" (I Corinthians 2:12). He also confirms in Galatians 4:6 that "because ye are sons, God hath sent forth the Spirit of his Son into your hearts, crying, Abba, Father." This indicates his indwelling the believer; and this indwelling power is necessary that we may walk well-pleasing to God in this present world. Someone has said, "Unless there is within us that which is above us, we shall soon yield to that which is about us."

The well-known passage in I Corinthians 12:13 asserts that we are baptized by the Spirit at conversion, and Galatians 3:27 also confirms this.

We are also sealed by the Spirit at conversion: "after that ye believed, ye were sealed with the Holy Spirit of promise" (Ephesians 1:13). This is further confirmed in II Corinthians 1:22.

3. *After conversion*, he fills, gives assurance, teaches, produces righteousness, controls our service, directs our worship, offers prayers, and bestows gifts.

Acts 4:31; 9:17; 13:9, 52 all tell of believers who were filled with the Holy Spirit. Ephesians 5:18 commands all believers to be filled with the Spirit.

To be filled with the Spirit is to manifest the purpose and power of God. Dr. F. E. Marsh says that

> An inert substance or a living body may become so surcharged and transformed with another force foreign to itself, that when we touch it we feel only the foreign force which fills it. Galvanize a pail of water, and then put your hand into it. You touch the water, but you feel only the electricity which pervades it. Take a bar of iron and put it into the fire. Soon the fire enters it, and takes possession of every atom of which it is com-

posed. If you touch it while red-hot you will scarcely feel the iron, but you will certainly feel the fire. So it is with a man when he is filled with God. Come near to him and touch him, and as you touch the man you feel God.

Speaking of the believer who seeks for the fulness of the Holy Spirit, Hudson Taylor declares,

> The Holy Spirit enters the heart, in his fulness, that can boast of nothing but an aching void. Maybe, no ecstasy, no rushing mighty wind, no fiery baptism, but nevertheless, "the Lord whom ye seek shall suddenly come to his temple." It is not striving after faith, but resting in the faithful One!

F. B. Meyer once said,

> If there is a man who needs the power of the Holy Spirit to rest upon him, it is I; but I do not know how to receive him. A voice said to me, "As you took forgiveness from the hand of the dying Christ, take the Holy Ghost from the hand of the living Christ." I turned to Christ and said, "Lord, I breathe in this whiff of warm night air, so I breathe into every part of me thy blessed Spirit." I felt no hand laid upon my head; and there was no lambent flame; there was no rushing sound from heaven; but by faith, without emotion, I took, and took for the first time, and I have kept on taking ever since.

I John 3:24 and Romans 8:16 affirm that the Holy Spirit will always give the believer assurance for every circumstance. This, again, is so our service may be made perfect. Dr. Jowett has said that the Holy Spirit does not comfort us to make us comfortable, but to make us comforters. We may not influence others until first of all we have assurance for ourselves.

His teaching ministry is revealed in John 16:13-14, I Corinthians 2:10, and I John 2:27. It is the Holy Spirit who interprets for us the word of God.

The Holy Spirit produces righteousness in us (Romans 8:2, 4, 13; Galatians 5:16-18). Galatians 5:22-23 lists the fruits of the Spirit: love, joy, peace, longsuffering, gentleness, goodness, faith, meekness, and temperance. As his righteousness is produced in us, we come to abhor sin as he hates it; for his hatred for sin is the hatred of snow for soot, of salvation for sin, of righteousness for revelry, of good for greed, of sanity for savagery, of truth for treachery, of virtue for vulgarity.

The Holy Spirit thus controls our service and directs our actions (Acts 16:6-7, 9). Various gifts are bestowed upon the Lord's servants by the Spirit (I Corinthians 12:4-11), in order that we may effectively serve him.

A seminarian saw an old lady attempting to cross a busy intersection and offered to help her. "Just trust me," he said. "Put your hand on my arm and I will guide you across safely."

When they were safely across, the aged one remarked, "You are a good boy. Are you a Christian?"

"Oh, yes," was the reply. "I am studying for the gospel ministry."

"You remind me of the Holy Spirit," was her quick rejoinder.

"Please, ma'am, don't compare me with such a high and holy One," the student protested.

She replied, "You have done for me just what the Holy Spirit desires to do for every Christian. He came into the world to walk alongside of the Christian and to keep him away from all harm, and lead him in the paths that are right."

We are also reminded that acceptable worship must be in the Spirit (John 4:23-24; Philippians 3:3). Much of our so-called worship becomes mechanical because there is an evident lack of dependence upon the Spirit. This is not true worship.

Again, in our praying, the Spirit makes interecession for us (Romans 8:26-27). Jude 20 admonishes us to pray in the Holy Spirit, for it is only such praying that will bring conviction to the hearts of the unconverted.

Newman Hall stood one morning on Mount Snowden in Wales, with 120 others who had come to see the sun rise. Dr. Hall was invited to preach to those assembled; however, he was momentarily overcome with the sunrise and he was unable to preach. Instead, he poured out his soul in prayer. As a result, a great stillness enveloped the group, and when he had finished praying they quietly went their various ways. Sometime later, Dr. Hall was told that forty people had been converted that morning and every one of them had united with the church. "But I didn't preach to them," Dr. Hall exclaimed in surprise. "I only prayed." His informer replied, "Yes, and more wonderful still, they did not understand a word you said. None of them could understand English; they only knew Welsh."

Such is the work of the Holy Spirit.